599 WIL 1996

WITHDRAWN

D1442425

National Audubon Society
Book of WILD ANIMALS

WINGS BOOKS
New York • Avenel, New Jersey

National Audubon Society
Book of WILD ANIMALS

Edited by Les Line and Edward R. Ricciuti

This 1996 edition is published by Wings Books,
a division of Random House Value Publishing, Inc.,
40 Engelhard Avenue, Avenel, New Jersey 07001,
by arrangement with Chanticleer Press, Inc.,
568 Broadway, Suite 1005A, New York, New York 10012.

Wings Books and colophon are trademarks of Random House Value Publishing, Inc.

National Audubon Society® is a registered trademark of National Audubon Society, Inc.
All rights reserved.

Random House
New York • Toronto • London • Sydney • Auckland

Printed and bound in the United States of America

Library of Congress Cataloging-in-Publication Data

National Audubon Society book of wild animals / edited by Les Line and
    Edward R. Ricciuti.
        p.   cm.
    Rev. ed of: The Audubon Society book of wild animals / Les Line
and Edward Ricciuti. New York : H.N. Abrams, 1977.
    ISBN 0-517-14945-1
    1. Mammals.   I. Line, Les.   II. Ricciuti, Edward R.
III. National Audubon Society.   IV. Audubon Society book of wild
animals.
QL706.N235   1996
599—dc20   96-3915
                                                                            CIP

8 7 6 5 4 3 2 1

Contents

National Audubon Society

The mission of the NATIONAL AUDUBON SOCIETY is to conserve and restore natural ecosystems, focusing on birds, other wildlife, and their habitats for the benefit of humanity and the earth's biological diversity.

In the vanguard of the environmental movement, AUDUBON has more than 550,000 members, 14 regional and state offices, and an extensive chapter network in the United States and Latin America, plus a professional staff of scientists, lobbyists, lawyers, policy analysts, and educators.

Through our nationwide sanctuary system we manage 150,000 acres of critical wildlife habitat and unique natural areas for birds, wild animals, and rare plant life.

Our award-winning *Audubon* magazine, published six times a year and sent to all members, carries outstanding articles and color photography on wildlife and nature, and presents in-depth reports on critical environmental issues, as well as conservation news and commentary. We also publish *Field Notes,* a journal reporting on seasonal bird sightings continent-wide, and *Audubon Adventures,* a bimonthly children's newsletter reaching nearly 500,000 students.

Our acclaimed *World of Audubon* television documentaries on TBS deal with a variety of environmental themes, while our children's series for The Disney Channel, *Audubon's Animals,* introduces family audiences to endangered species of wildlife. Other Audubon film and television projects include conservation-oriented movies and educational videos. The NATIONAL AUDUBON SOCIETY also sponsors books and electronic programs on nature, plus travel programs to exotic places like Antarctica, Africa, Australia, Baja California, Galapagos Islands, Indonesia, and Patagonia.

For information about how you can become a member, please write or call:

NATIONAL AUDUBON SOCIETY
Membership Department
700 Broadway
New York, New York 10003
212/979–3000

For Charles H. Callison,
spokesman for the Audubon cause

Preface

"Free as a mammal." Somehow it doesn't sound right. Yet that statement is no less correct than "Free as a bird." Therein lies an irony.

The passions and sentiments that mammals arouse in man bridge the gamut of human emotions—affection, love, envy, awe, fear, hate. But these feelings are almost entirely in response to particular kinds of mammals—dogs, for instance, or bears—or even to individuals. Not to mammals as a group.

We talk collectively about birds as though there is no difference between an ostrich, a penguin, and a hummingbird. It is "the birds" that sing, and "the birds" that build nests. Whether a person goes afield to observe warblers, hawks, or geese, he or she is a "bird watcher." The term is in the dictionary. But try looking for "mammal watcher." There simply is no word for the person who walks to the meadow in the evening to wait for deer, or enjoys the antics of squirrels in the park, or follows the trail of a hunting fox in the snow.

Nor do mammals enjoy the broad popular appeal of birds. Nearly every town of at least modest size has its local bird club. Great organizations like the National Audubon Society, the Royal Society for the Protection of Birds, and the International Council for Bird Preservation owe their birth to the delight people share in birds.

Feeding birds has become a phenomenon of our times. Designers labor over new devices to dispense the tons of bird seed sold annually. But few people feed wild mammals, except casually or unintentionally—the raccoon that comes to the back door for a handout, or the squirrel that commandeers the bird feeder.

Field guides to the birds are abundant, field guides to the mammals few indeed. Bird watchers go to great extremes and expense to add new species to their "life lists." Few nature enthusiasts keep track of the different mammals they have seen and identified. Birds are the subject of innumerable paeans and poems, mammals of a handful. Few mammals inspire the superlatives we accord the passing of a flight of swans, the

OPPOSITE. *This young alpaca (Lama pacos) has been selectively bred for the long wool that will be sheared from its sides when it matures—a wool of unmatched quality that will be made into coats costing several thousand dollars. Once, garments of alpaca were worn only by Inca royalty.*

11

dive of a hunting falcon, the song of a thrush. If any single point of view dominates our attitude toward mammals, it is that their worth is determined by their utility. And this has not worked out particularly well for the mammals. There is nothing intrinsically wrong with using what nature provides. The problem arises when reasonable or necessary use becomes exploitation, when greed jeopardizes survival.

Some birds, of course, are hunted for sport or food. A few have been domesticated. Others are caged for the beauty of their form, color, or song. It is also true that man is responsible for the extinction of the passenger pigeon, the Carolina parakeet, the great auk, and others, either deliberately or indirectly through the destruction of habitat. And near the turn of this century, the plumed birds were nearly wiped out to provide feathers for women's hats.

By and large, however, our attitude toward birdlife has been sympathetic, if not reverent.

The mammals have been less fortunate. They are valued not for what they are, but for what they can do for man. Can they be ridden, harnessed, petted, eaten, or are their skins or tusks precious? Worse, many mammals are considered a threat to our prosperity. Although the Indians of the North American plains prized and revered the buffalo, to the settlers who poured into the West after the Civil War the great shaggy beast was an enemy. Not only did it take rangeland needed for livestock or crops, it provided food and comfort to the Indian foe. And, of course, its hide and meat were marketable. Thus sixty million buffalo were slaughtered in a few years; often only the tongue was salvaged. In 1875, the Texas legislature met at Austin to discuss a bill for the protection of the fast-shrinking buffalo herds. General Phil Sheridan, charged by the U.S. Army with subjugating the southwestern Indians, testified against the proposal:

"Let them kill, skin, and sell until the buffalo is exterminated, as it is the only way to bring about a lasting peace and allow civilization to advance."

Dozens of mammals have been exploited just as destructively. Millions of fur seals, sea otters, and beavers were killed for their pelts with little concern for the future. The luxury fur trade was responsible for the near demise of many of the spotted cats of Asia and Africa. In another kind of exploitation, but equally devastating, the populations of many primates, like the orangutan, have been reduced to dangerously low levels by the capture of animals for the pet, zoo, and laboratory trade.

Why do we view mammals so restrictively, as compared with birds? Is it because birds are beautiful, emblazoned with brilliant colors, and so graceful? Is it because their songs herald spring and have inspired great composers to write lovely music? Is it because we are envious of their power of flight, their ability to vanish into the clouds, to soar as if they had no link with the earth, to hurtle from the heavens with incredible speed? But pause and consider, please. Is the plumage of any bird more brilliant than the blue and scarlet on the face of a mandrill? Lovelier than the amber, black, and white that stamp the tiger? Is any bird more graceful than a racing dolphin?

Song? From podiums high in the rain forests of Southeast Asia, the gibbons make music that is as haunting as any sound in nature. Its magic was described in *Wild Heritage* by Sally Carrighar, who followed the gibbon song as it rose "by halftone steps to exactly the height of an octave, where the voices trilled with great flexibility. Each tone was introduced by a grace note, the keynote E, and the whole up-flung roulade had the effect of expressing triumphant joy. At the top, during

Largest of its kind is the South African porcupine (Hystrix africae australis). *But the angry rattling of its five-inch tail, covered with long white spines, does not deter local hunters, who prize its flesh.*

the trill, the gibbons quivered through all their bodies. Finally they let the song ease away in a few diminishing quarter-notes."

No less stirring is the cry of a wolf echoing across the Alaskan tundra, or the bugling of an elk on a chilly autumn evening in a Rocky Mountain meadow.

Flight? More than any other attribute, this is the one most closely associated with birds—although not all birds fly, and many species fly with merely modest skills. However, several mammals—flying squirrels and the marsupial opossums of Australia—engage in swooping glides which are spectacular examples of unpowered flight. And one out of seven of all living species of mammals—the vast order of bats—is capable of powered flight with speed and maneuverability to equal nearly any bird.

In truth, the answer to the great appeal of birds may lie in the fact that they are so evident, while the human experience with mammals is limited. Most birds are active by day, and one can see birds in considerable numbers even in the heart of a city. Mammals, in contrast, are generally nocturnal or crepuscular and retreat into concealment when the sun rises. Most of them shun people and civilization. Even when they coexist in close proximity with man, they are adept at staying out of sight of their neighbors. John Kieran, in his book *Natural History of New York City,* describes how even a great metropolis can harbor myriad mammals whose presence is hardly suspected: "As for 'wild animals' within the city limits," Kieran writes, "New York has a far larger population of wild quadrupeds than most of the resident bipeds suspect. That's because so many of the wild mammals are small in size and nocturnal in habit, as a result of which they are rarely seen except by those who look for them."

Of course, a few mammals can be observed in multitudes by day—the fur seals which gather in immense colonies, or herbivores such as the wildebeests which form large herds on the African plains. But they are restricted to dwindling havens far from the masses of humanity.

The mammals deserve to be celebrated and treasured for all their magic and mystery, for their fascinating modes of living, and for the curiosities among them. This book provides some insights into their life and lore, and examines certain unusual facts about them, but it is not a treatise on biology. Rather, it is a tribute to the mammals, applauding them for their wonder and their accomplishments. It is our means, through the great photographs of mammals to be found in the world, of awakening greater public interest in their ways and, ultimately, in their survival.

Edward R. Ricciuti

OPPOSITE. *This young chimpanzee* (Pan troglodytes) *may suckle its mother for the first four years of its life and will remain at her side for several more years. It will not breed until it is at least eleven years old. Believed to be the most intelligent animal next to man, chimps have a vocal repertoire of thirty-two different sounds and are able to use simple tools. Though predominantly vegetarian, they occasionally kill small antelopes and even monkeys.*

National Audubon Society
Book of WILD ANIMALS

Life in the Trees

From the ground, the animals that teem in the forest canopy of Southeast Asia are largely invisible, but a multitude of sounds reveals their presence in the tangle of leaves and lianas. Myriad small creatures chitter and chatter. And in the cool of the early morning, as well as the shadowed hours of the late afternoon, the gibbons begin to call, often from perches in the loftiest crowns of trees. Their melodious whoops ring through the green galleries, echoing from the arboreal world above, a haunting reminder that all of the primate tribe, even those which walk with two legs on the ground, have been shaped and indelibly stamped by life in the trees.

Developing from primitive, arboreal, shrewlike mammals that arose while the dinosaurs still walked the land, many primates quickly found their niche in the branches. Man and a few large monkeys such as the mandrill and the gorilla live for the most part on the ground, but there are times when even they show an affinity for the trees—gorillas often will construct a nest of vegetation in the branches and go to sleep in it.

Adaptation to arboreal living has been most refined in the now endangered gibbons, including the siamang, most agile of all mammals in the boughs. In the canopy, siamangs fling themselves into the void between branches with hair-raising abandon, arresting their flight by hooking elongate hands around limb or liana, then hurling themselves into space again.

The ability to wrap a hand around a limb and grasp it—to hold on to something—is a superb advantage for a creature living in the trees, and began to appear almost at the outset of primate existence. Claws slowly changed to flattened nails and long, sensitive digits. Eventually, as a thumb opposable to the other digits developed, the primate hand became capable of such delicate maneuvers as picking up a twig and probing for insects within a termite mound, something that chimpanzees accomplish with ease. Using hands and fingers—and feet and toes—in the branches was demanding to the visual organs.

19

THIS PAGE AND OPPOSITE. *For the first three or four months of its life, an infant savanna baboon* (Papio cynocephalus) *hangs upside down beneath its mother's belly, clinging to her breast. But soon it will try to ride on her back, holding tightly with hands and feet until it masters the trick of sitting near her rump, its tiny back braced against the female's stiffly held tail. When she runs, however, the youngster will lie flat. A mother and her newborn infant are the immediate focus of interest in a baboon troop: dominant males hover about and other females groom both the baby and the mother. Old males also play with young baboons, pulling their tails or letting the infants leap on them.*

Gradually, over the course of evolution, the eyes moved from the sides of the head to the front, providing better depth perception and eventually the ability to see the world in three dimensions. The gray cortex of the brain not only grew in bulk but gained more surface area for multiplying cells by wrinkling until it was covered with folds and convolutions.

The evolution of primate history over more than 70 million years is reflected—although by no means exactly—by the primates that roam the tropics and their margins today. The earliest primate probably resembled today's tree shrews of India and Southeast Asia. By 50 million years ago, primates of a more advanced type than tree shrews flourished over a vast portion of the earth. These were the prosimians, whose eyes faced forward, or nearly so, and whose hands and feet bore slender, flexible digits. Today, similar forms in the suborder *Prosimii* still survive in the jungles, or on islands where they were free of competition and predation. Madagascar is the home of the endangered aye-aye, the lemurs, and the indri. The lorises and pottos inhabit Asia and Africa, respectively. Galagos, or bushbabies, are also African, whereas the diminutive, saucer-eyed tarsiers haunt the forests of the Philippines and the Indonesian region.

To watch a South American squirrel monkey manipulate a grape, turning it round and round in its fingers, cocking its head and following the soft little sphere with its eyes, is to know how far the monkeys and apes have come from their shrew-like ancestors. Binocular color vision makes the world a different place for them, and fingers capable of fine, independent movement, together with a relatively gigantic brain, permit exploration of that world.

When the graceful, long-limbed spider monkey dangles from a liana in the South American forest, its sensitive prehensile tail serving as a fifth hand, it testifies along with the gibbons that the primates have attained nearly absolute mastery over the arboreal environment.

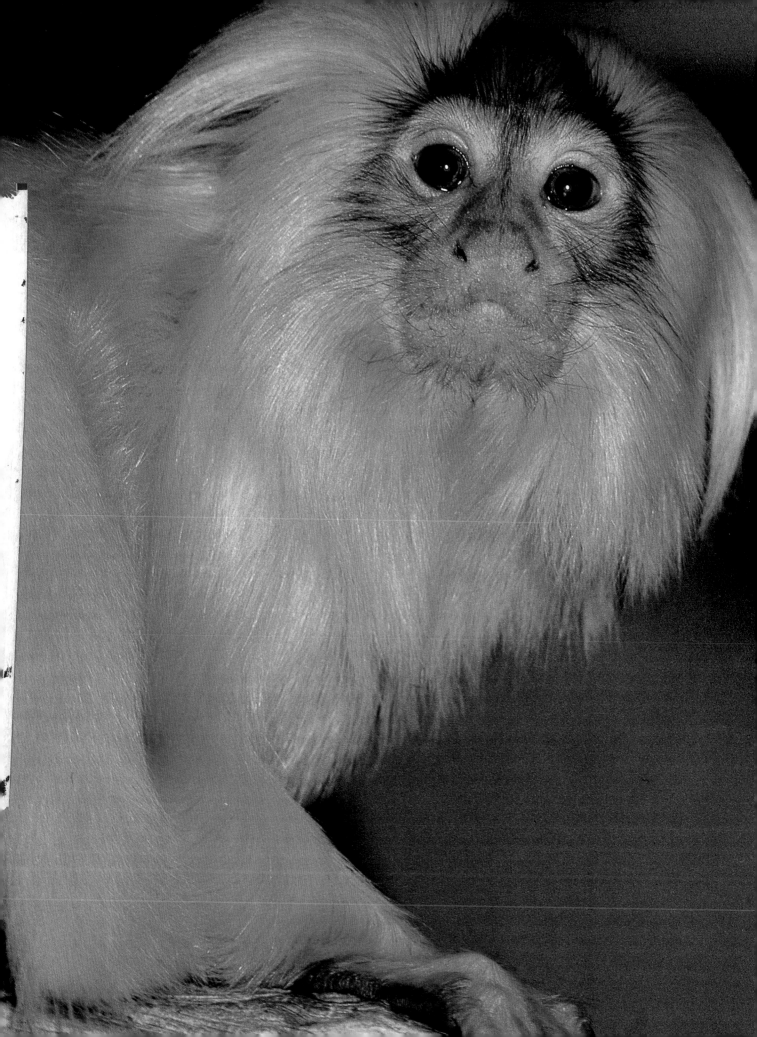

OVERLEAF. *THIS PAGE AND OPPOSITE. No other monkeys live as far north as the population of Japanese macaques (Macaca fuscata) at the tip of the island of Honshu. There, in winter, five feet of snow covers the mountain slopes, forcing the leaf- and fruit-eating monkeys to subsist on tree buds, shoots, and bark. Japanese macaques are highly gregarious, forming societies in which the males are organized into a complex class system and even the females have social status. For instance, when foraging macaques stop to feed, they form two circles: the older males join the females, infants, and juveniles in the middle, with the young males making up the outer ring. Strictly protected by the Japanese government, this is the monkey that symbolizes the wisdom of Buddha: "See no evil, hear no evil, speak no evil."*

OVERLEAF. With remarkably long arms, and hands that do not grasp a branch but are used like hooks, the white-handed gibbon (Hylobates lar) swings through the rain forests of Malaysia in a blur. Gibbons are the most agile of all primates—indeed, of all mammals—and may cover ten feet in a single swing. Their populations, however, have been decimated by logging of their habitat and by the relentless pet trade in Southeast Asia; young gibbons are captured by killing the mothers.

The descent of the apes to the ground, and their first explorations of the savanna, is an epic forever lost; but glimpses of what it must have been like emerge from watching the meanderings of bands of rhesus monkeys over the landscape of southern Asia, and gelada baboons romping on the rocky heights of Ethiopia.

The baboon troop is a society on the move, not haphazardly, but in precisely organized fashion. Baboon troops are governed by scrupulously observed patterns of complex social behavior. Within the baboon troop, for example, a youngster assumes new responsibilities with age. Baboon society is above all cohesive, a trait very much suited to survival. As long as the troop is together, no single baboon need face alone a threat from an outside enemy. Breeding male chimpanzees may also threaten aggressors in united fashion, although their groups are not as large or quite so organized as those of the baboons. Male chimpanzees have sometimes been observed working together in another way; they will surround a monkey while a larger male moves in and kills it for food. Most primates, perhaps with the notable exception of the forest-dwelling gorilla, will at least sample bird's eggs, nestlings, insects, and other small prey. Life on the savanna, however, the mode of living that was to produce the first humans, carries primate predation to the ultimate—the stalking and killing of game and the consumption of raw flesh.

Marsupial Marvels

A creature moves in the treetops crowning a ridge in the lush forest of northeastern Australia. Brown of fur, with a two-foot-long body and an even longer, cylindrical tail, the animal quickly nibbles leaves high above the forest floor. Then, for reasons unknown, it decides it must get to the ground—in a hurry. It launches itself into space, tail streaming behind as a rudder, and sails through the air for almost fifty feet. Once the prodigious leap to the earth has been completed, the creature rises to a half crouch and hops into the shadows, now moving much like any other kangaroo.

The tree kangaroos offer dramatic evidence of how the marsupials have diverged as they have adapted to a remarkably wide range of living conditions. In Australia, from which most of the more advanced mammals are absent, the marsupials have taken advantage of the niches left by the lack of competition. Their varying approaches to survival are expressed even in their wide range of body sizes. Consider the gulf between the minuscule planigales, which feed on grasshoppers longer than they, and the great gray kangaroo, which is the size of a large man.

As a rule, however, marsupials share a basic body plan. They have longer hind legs than forelegs, and many have a distinctive taper to their hind parts, and a thick-based tail, a characteristic normally associated with reptiles.

Of course, the external trait most commonly associated with the marsupials—and, in fact, their trademark—is the pouch. Opening to the front in some, to the rear in others, the pouch is a halfway house between the womb and the outside world. When the marsupial is born, it is ill-prepared for life independent of its mother's body. While in the womb, the embryonic marsupial does not have the benefit of the strong placental connection to the uterine wall that nourishes the developing young of more advanced mammals until they are fully formed. The marsupial, therefore, is born before it is fully developed. Unable to see, it still must negotiate its way through its mother's fur to the pouch.

OPPOSITE. *The tiny feathertail glider (Acrobates pygmaeus) of eastern Australia is less than seven inches long, including its tail. Feeding on sap, nectar, insects, leaves, and blossoms, it can glide 80 feet, using its peculiar tail to slow and steer aeriel paths around tree trunks before landing.*

OVERLEAF. *At top speed, a red kangaroo (Macropus rufus) can dash across the Australian plains at 35 miles an hour, covering twenty-five feet with each leap. If hard-pressed, a female kangaroo's pouch muscles may loosen, and her joey may fall from the pouch and be lost to a predator.*

33

That is the most hazardous journey the marsupial ever makes, and not all make it. Once inside, however, the youngster has the shelter, warmth, and food it needs to grow to a fully formed creature.

Beyond its basic characteristics, the marsupial body has considerable range. The peculiarities of each form provide clues to the way of life for which it has evolved. The stocky, badger-like body of the wombat is built for burrowing. The koala, whose rotund body has been immortalized in the form of the teddy bear, has long flexible fingers tipped with hooked claws for life in the trees.

Myriad smaller marsupials, which scurry about the ground like mice and rats, have bodies that outwardly resemble those of such rodents. Several groups of tiny carnivorous marsupials, such as the dunnarts and the Kultarrs and wuhl-wuhls, are, in fact, commonly known as "marsupial mice." And, in an illustration of turnabout being

LEFT. *Not a true cat but a marsupial carnivore, the rare western native cat* (Dasyurus geoffroii) *hunts the Australian forests at night for small mammals and birds, such as the parrot on which it is feeding. The native cat may produce as many as eighteen young, but only those that find one of the six teats will survive.*

fair play, just as there are kangaroo rats among the rodents, the marsupials have rat kangaroos. The smallest, the musky rat kangaroo of Queensland, is less than a foot, not counting its tail.

The kangaroos show how in Australia, and partly in New Guinea, marsupials have moved into niches occupied in other places by the placental mammals. The great gray kangaroo, the red kangaroo, and the euro are browsers and grazers, playing the role that four-footed herbivores assume elsewhere. Each of these large kangaroos specializes in a particular type of habitat. The gray leaps through parklike forests and bush country. The red is a creature of vast inland plains. The euro stays among the rocks, and can survive in sun-baked badlands shunned by its fellow kangaroos.

As demonstrated by the tree kangaroos, the marsupials have extended their colonization of habitats into the branches. The cuscuses, saucer-eyed, nocturnal creatures which range as far as Celebes and the

Solomon Islands, live entirely in the trees and, like a number of other marsupials, have a prehensile tail. The greater gliding possum of eastern Australia's high timber, have even evolved flaps of loose skin along the sides of their bodies, so that they can glide, like flying squirrels, from limb to limb.

As predators, marsupials have exploited myriad possibilities, many of which mirror the roles of the true carnivores. Only two relatively large marsupial predators remain in the Australian region, however, and they are restricted to Tasmania. One, fairly common, is the Tasmanian devil, a feisty beast that is built like a mini-bear, with a head that seems as large as its twenty-pound body and gives the impression of being all muscle and teeth. It might be dubbed the marsupial hyena, because it prowls by night, sometimes making unearthly noises, and scavenges carcasses, using its bone-crushing bite to good advantage.

All of the Australian marsupials may have originated from an omnivorous form, similar to today's American opossums. During the final stages of the Age of Reptiles, more than 70 million years ago, marsupials arose in North or South America and could have reached Australia via Africa or Antarctica.

Today, the opossums and a virtually unknown family of shrewlike creatures called "rat opossums" are the only survivors of the competition the placental mammals brought to South America about 5 million years ago. But as befits survivors of a difficult battle, they are hardy and adaptable. The Virginia opossum has even turned the tables by extending its range into the heart of North America. It has pushed as far north as Canada, and the only real problem it has faced is frostbite on its naked ears and tail in very cold weather. It adapts so well to humans that it readily inhabits heavily populated urban areas, even venturing into New York City.

Although the marsupials begin life at a great disadvantage in their competition with the placental mammals, and the domain of the kangaroo and its kin has diminished, the pouched mammals remain testimony to the marvelous flexibility of nature.

RIGHT. *The spotted cuscus* (Spilocuscus maculatus) *is a monkey-like marsupial that inhabits forests from the Cape York Peninsula, Australia, to New Guinea and islands as far as Celebes and the Solomons. The cuscus moves sluggishly and eats quantities of leaves as well as small mammals and birds. Its prehensile tail is furred on top and naked and scaly below, and its tiny ears are hidden beneath woolly fur.*

OVERLEAF. *The familiar, slow-motion koala* (Phascolarctos cinereus) *spends much of its time wedged in a fork of a tree—asleep. It has no tail, and it may once have been a ground dweller, but curved claws, long arms, and a viselike grip ease its arboreal life. The koala gives birth to one young, which it raises in a pouch that opens backward.*

Mammals with Wings

Atop a jungled hill called Tamana, in the center of Trinidad, the earth opens a dark, jagged maw. The forest growing around the somber breach in the surface is lush and lively. Pecking after seeds on the ground, tinamous whistle, icy clear. Cicadas buzz warmly from hidden arboreal havens. Sunlight filters through the trees and dapples the red lobster-claw bracts that sheathe the tiny flowers of the *Heliconia* plants. Within that hole in the hilltop, however, the colors and music of the forest are extinguished, the light obscured by a lip of rock just below the rim. A dozen feet down, dimly seen and alive with tiny frogs, a slick, muddy floor slopes abruptly into abysmal gloom.

And from that gloom, should one trespass there, arises a sound like a whirlwind. It swirls up, as though from the black bowels of the planet, the sound of bad dreams and childhood fears. Vast and pervasive, the sound becomes one with the darkness, and as it mounts to a dry, leathery thunder, its source becomes clear. Wings make that sound, countless thousands of them, wings of membranous delicacy, moved by the cave's population of bats.

The sound of bat wings was first made more than 50 million years ago, at the dawn of the Age of Mammals, when bats very similar to those living today evolved the capability of powered flight. No other group of mammals has ever repeated that feat. For this, if no other reason, bats ought to be admired, yet they are abhorred almost universally by humans. A major exception seems to be the Chinese, who view bats as beneficent—the Chinese word for bat, *fu*, sounds identical to the character meaning happiness or good luck.

Western aversion to the bat stems from manifold roots. The probable reason that medieval artists equipped Satan and his demonic minions with bat wings, for instance, is that many kinds of bats roost in caves. Some bat caves, astoundingly, are tenanted by millions of the winged mammals, hanging upside down by the feet or wedged into crevices.

OPPOSITE. *Extraordinary among an extraordinary order of mammals is the common vampire bat (Desmodus rotundus),* which inhabits both deserts and tropical forests from northern Mexico into Chile and Argentina. Its diet is exclusively blood! On its nocturnal forays, a vampire bat will consume forty percent of its own body weight in blood—about a tablespoon—during several nightly feedings from cows, horses, burros, deer, peccaries, or, on infrequent occasions, a sleeping human. Then it retires to a cave or hollow tree to digest its meal. A vampire alights on the ground and hops to its victim, slices into the skin with an almost painless bite, then laps at the blood with an in-and-out darting motion of its tongue. The bat's saliva contains an anticoagulant that keeps the blood flowing freely for the twenty-minute feeding period. Neither the bat's bite nor the loss of blood is serious, but vampires can transmit rabies and livestock diseases.

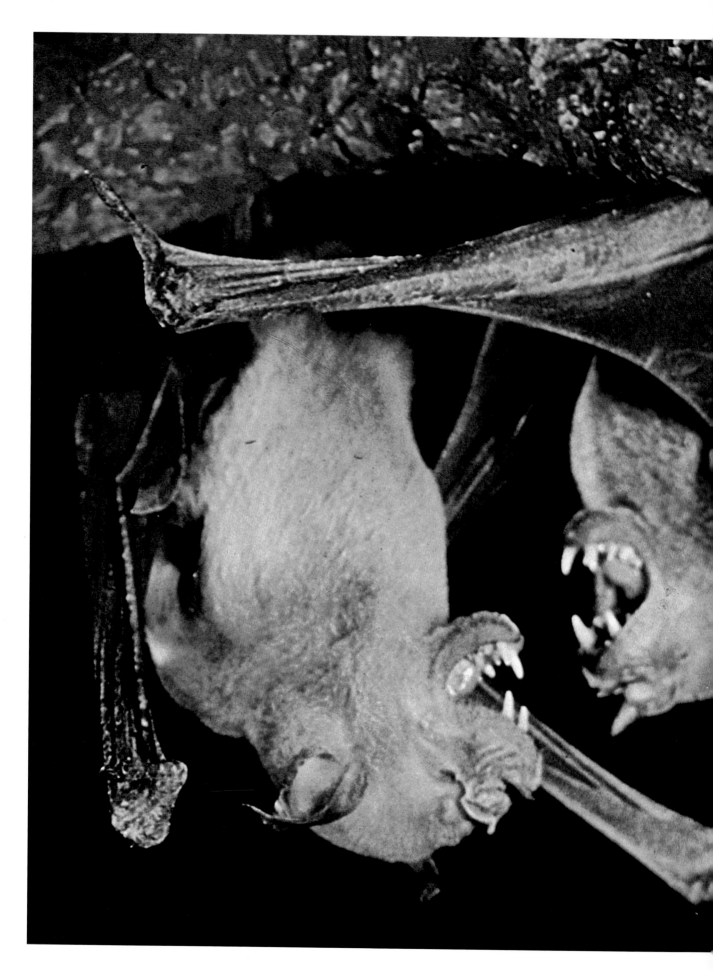

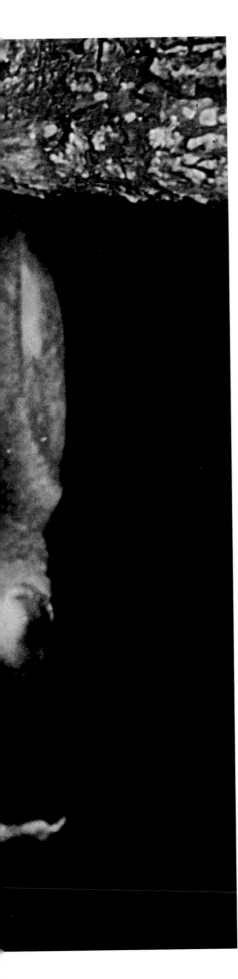

It also did the image of the bat no good when Cortez encountered species in tropical America that fed upon blood. The notion that a human bloodsucker could take the guise of a bat was quickly grafted upon the European vampire tradition. Because of the unsavory associations that have developed around it, the bat has been treated with a loathing directed at no other mammal and usually reserved for scaly or many-legged things that creep and crawl.

Not surprisingly, fear has blinded people to the truly splendid creature that is the bat, especially in view of the spectacular diversity of its more than 900 different species.

Giants among the bats are the Old World fruit eaters, some of which carry their rabbit-sized bodies on wings measuring almost seven feet from tip to tip. From such strapping creatures, bats range in size all the way down to the minuscule Philippine bamboo bat, which has a body less than two inches long. This winged Lilliputian roosts snuggled within the hollow of a bamboo stem, clinging to the walls of its refuge with suckers on its feet. It belongs to a vast family, almost global in distribution, which includes the North American little brown bats, big brown bats, and pipistrelles. They are the bane of insects that fly at dusk and by night, which the bats pursue, wings a-blur, in zigzag chases through the air. Insects, however, are not the only creatures that fall prey to bats; some bats eat such unlikely victims as shrimp, frogs, and even one another.

Blood alone is the diet of the true vampires, however, three species that belong to the family Desmodontidae. These bats can digest no other food. They feed, not by sucking, as commonly believed, but by lapping up the blood with feverish speed. The wound from which the vampire draws its sustenance is slight, a tiny scoop of skin nicked out by razor-edged upper incisors. So deft and painless is the cut, it seldom awakens sleeping victims, human or animal.

LEFT. *Having roosted too close to each other, two Commerson's leaf-nosed bats* (Hipposideros commersoni) *attack with bared fangs, flailing arms, and ultrasonic shrieks. Damage from such fights, however, is rare. This species feasts mostly on insects, caught on the wing; but beetle larvae, dug out of the pulp of wild fig fruits, are also an important part of their diet. The leaf-nosed bat's noseleaf — an elaborate growth on the nose — lets the bat focus a beam of ultrasound from the nose as the bat moves its head from side to side, searching for insects. Some echo-locating bats emit the beam through the mouth; they do not have a noseleaf.*

THIS PAGE AND OPPOSITE. *The fishing bulldog bat* (Noctilio leporinus) *of Central and South America is a skilled fisher of both fresh and salt water. Raking the surface with long claws, it gaffs a small fish, swiftly lifts the catch to its mouth, and either eats it on the wing or chops the fish into pieces, storing them in its cheeks for later consumption. In late afternoon, numbers of chirping bulldog bats may be seen zigzagging over the surf in the company of brown pelicans, gleaning small fish stirred up by the big birds. Scientists think that these bats echolocate fish that are close enough to the surface of the water to cause ripples.*

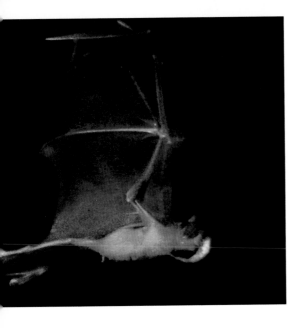

More palatable, perhaps, to the human way of thinking are the feeding habits of the flower bats. The nectar-feeding bat flits through the jungles of Central and South America, stopping to tap flowers for their sweet fluid. It can get at the nectar of even deep, vaselike blooms, for its tongue is longer than its body. Blossoms also draw some of the huge Old World fruit bats, which unfortunately do not merely drink but masticate the blooms to a pulp.

The giant fruit bats, in addition to size, are characterized by their long-snouted, doglike faces, and eyes that are large and luminous. Internally, they share another trait which, along with their big eyes, reveals an important fact about the way they live. The part of the brain devoted to vision occupies approximately the same amount of space as the portion concerned with hearing—in direct contrast to the other bats, in whose brains auditory areas have expanded vastly at the expense of those concerned with vision. The differences in brain structure relate directly to the fact that all the fruit bats orient themselves visually, whereas other bats use sound. Indeed, most bats have a natural sonar that enables them to navigate by what scientists call echolocation. The bats literally talk themselves toward a target, or around obstacles, by assessing the echoes of high-pitched sounds broadcast by their larynxes and bounced off the target. When engaged in aerial pursuit or other tricky maneuvers, they may emit pulses at the buzz-saw tempo of 200 per second.

The wings that carry bats through the air are composed of only two layers of skin, tightly framed upon limbs resembling delicate, elongated finger bones. Powered by muscles in the chest, the seemingly fragile wings can loft bats as high as 10,000 feet and take them on seasonal migrations of 1,000 miles. Some other mammals, as we have seen, can sail through the air, but ultimately they are bound to the earth. The bats, however, by virtue of having true wings, have added another dimension to the mammalian domination of the earth. They have conquered the skies.

OPPOSITE. *By ramming its snout into the corolla, an impatient Mexican long-nosed bat has forced open a flower on the tree-like saguaro cactus. Bats are important pollinators of the night-blooming saguaro, which in turn is an important source of nourishment for the bats. A single blossom, jutting safely beyond the spines of the cactus, can produce a tablespoon of sugary nectar.*

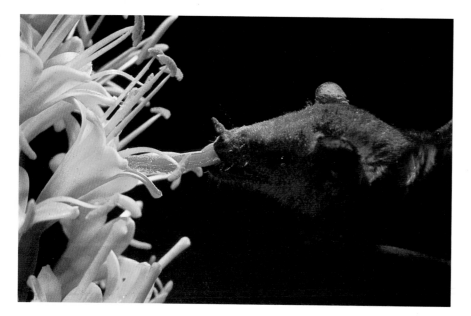

LEFT. *A hovering long-nosed bat* (Leptonycteris nivalis) *reaches deep within the flowers of an agave in search of pollen. Hundreds of thousands of long-nosed bats migrate between Arizona and Mexico, following the blooming season of desert plants.*

OVERLEAF. *Crammed together in a Kentucky cave, thousands of little brown bats (*Myotis lucifugus*) hibernate through the cold winter months. Many of them flew hundreds of miles to reach this site. The bats of the genus* Myotis, *often called mouse-eared bats, are found everywhere in the world except Arctic and Antarctic regions and some mid-ocean islands. They hunt exclusively for insects, resting after a feeding flight to digest their catch.*

Gnawing Hordes

With typical rodent resourcefulness, a muskrat has built her nursery under the overturned hulk of a rowboat rotting beside a small backyard pond. Her five young hide beneath the old boat, their small bodies huddled together in a mound of glossy fur. Something approaches their shelter, something that is not their mother, but considerably larger, and heavy of foot. Daylight floods the interior of the nursery as the bow of the boat is lifted from the ground. Instantly, the heap of fur separates into five small forms which scatter in headlong flight. Their dispersal seems frantic, wildly haphazard, but actually the flight of the muskrats is entirely purposeful, the paths deliberate. Each route leads to the same goal, the water. The water is safety, security, and concealment, a refuge which ages of evolution have programmed them to seek when threatened.

The way the muskrat has so fully exploited a niche in the waters of ponds, lakes, streams, and wetlands demonstrates the remarkable breadth of rodent adaptability. In their astonishing success, rodents have become nearly global in range, and have adapted to virtually all habitats open to mammals except the sea and the air, although, to be sure, some, such as the American flying squirrels, make brief, unpowered forays into the sky. The rodents as a group constitute the majority of mammals living on this planet. In species alone the rodents are legion, their varieties numbering in the thousands.

Within this immense multitude are creatures as disparate as the semi-aquatic capybaras, tropical American beasts that can weigh more than 100 pounds, and the tiny Cape mole rat of Africa, which tunnels after tubers and rocks. Rodent habits run the gamut of possibilities. The giant naked-tailed rat of New Guinea climbs trees in search of coconuts. The North American pocket gophers burrow under plants and pull them down into their underground dining chambers. The water rat of Australasia kills and eats fish, crustaceans, lizards, birds, and even other rats.

Despite the seemingly great difference between them, rodents differ only superficially. No matter where and how they live, all have two

OPPOSITE. *Scourge of civilization, the house mouse (*Mus musculus*) has been transported everywhere that man lives, carrying human diseases, destroying crops, ruining food stores, invading homes. Yet this same hated pest, in its albino and domestic forms, is an invaluable tool in medical research, especially in the search for the causes of and a cure for cancer.*

LEFT. *To get a better view of a prowling fox, an Arctic hare* (Lepus arcticus) *stands on its hind legs. This inhabitant of the Far North, from Greenland to Alaska, is wonderfully adapted to its harsh environment. Its winter pelage is snow white except for the black tips of the ears. The silky outer fur and thick woolly underfur provide a dense coat that does not part in the constant wind. Its large feet are heavily padded with stiff hair. Strong nails dig through frozen snow to expose twigs and roots of willows, sedges, and saxifrages, which are extracted with projecting incisors that operate like forceps. In storms, the Arctic hare digs a tunnel in the snow for shelter. On Canada's high Arctic islands, these gregarious animals form herds numbering several hundred.*

BELOW. *With a loud, sharp call, a black-tailed prairie dog* (Cynomys ludovicianus) *of the Great Plains of North America throws its forepaws high into the air and arches its head backward. Behaviorists call this display the "jump-yip." It usually means that the prairie dog making the display is advertising to neighbors that this territory is off-limits to them.*

ABOVE. *The world's most primitive rodent is the mountain beaver (Aplodontia rufa) of the rain- and fog-soaked coastal forests from northern California into British Columbia. Sometimes known by the name given it by Chinook Indians, sewellel, the mountain beaver is not closely related to a beaver, does not behave like a beaver, and rarely lives high in the mountains. About fifteen inches long, it resembles a tailless muskrat, digs elaborate burrow systems, and eats about any kind of plant material, from berries to ferns to evergreen needles.*

BELOW. *An inhabitant of coniferous forests and tundra across northwestern Canada and Alaska, and from Siberia to Norway, the northern red-backed vole (Clethrionomys rutilus) is active day or night the year around, gathering and storing tender vegetation, seeds, bark, lichens, fungus, and insects.*

pairs of curving incisor teeth, chisel sharp, which grow throughout their lives. One pair juts out from the lower jaw, the other directly above, so that in normal use they wear against each other, keeping the edges of the teeth keen.

Gnawing incisors are also the trademark of another group, successful in their own right but not on such an impressive scale as the rodents. These animals, the rabbits and hares and the little pikas, are born with three sets of upper incisors, although they retain only two pairs as adults.

With its incisors, the rodent can gnaw through the hardest shells, seed hulls, and rinds to get at the soft food within. The nemesis of man, the brown rat, can chew through metal sheeting or cinder block to get at human food stores. The beaver, using the upper incisors as a brace against the trunk and shaving away at the wood with the lower pair, can fell a tree in minutes.

The sharp-edged incisors also serve as a defensive weapon, which can be wielded with murderous results. The vicious bites of a cornered rat have made more than one attacker regret the choice of opponent. The hamster is known for its slashing attacks when aroused. Generally, however, rodents prefer not to do battle but to rely for safety on their ability to remain inconspicuous. As is known by anyone who has a pet hamster or gerbil, or whose house walls are a winter refuge for scurrying troops of deer mice, it is the night that brings forth the rodent hordes. In southern Africa, white-tailed rats skitter through the darkness over open areas, foraging for seeds. On the deserts of western North America, kangaroo rats emerge from their labyrinthine burrows to dance like elves upon the sand. In the swamps of South America, fish-eating rats course along the waterways.

There are a few rodents which, unlike their kin, sleep at night and are abroad by day. The woodchuck and the hoary marmot—a large ground squirrel—emerge from their cavernous burrows to feed by day and even sun themselves for hours at a time, seldom far from their underground havens. Hoary marmots, gregarious creatures that live in colonies from Alaska to Idaho, rely upon one of their number to serve as a sentinel when they are feeding. The sight of an eagle or a coyote will evoke a shrill warning whistle from the sentry, which sends all the marmots scurrying for their holes. Similarly, the earsplitting crash of the spatulate tail of a frightened beaver slapping the water will trigger a rush away from the shore and shallows by all beavers within hearing.

When it comes to the survival of the rodents as a group, however, it is not the ability to keep from being eaten that really matters, but rather their reproductive powers, which are unmatched among mammals. Consider the cotton rat. In its usual life span of about a year it may produce several litters of up to a dozen young each. Among the equally fecund rabbits and hares, the American cottontails produce up to five litters of about a half dozen young each in the space of a year. The true

rabbit of the Old World, ancestor of all domestic varieties, is fertile for more than a dozen years, if allowed to live that long, and on the average has more than ten young every year.

Not surprisingly, in view of their reproductive abilities, various species among the gnawing hordes experience cyclic population bulges. Lemmings multiply immensely over a cycle of three or four years, until their food supply no longer can sustain them. The buildup of lemming populations triggers mass migrations of the small rodents, particularly in Scandinavia. Driven by an unyielding urge to move on, a flood of lemmings sweeps out of the hinterlands in a mindless crush that apparently has no goal but to keep traveling. For most of the lemmings in the swarm, the journey ends only in the claws or jaws of predators, or in the chill waters of rivers or lakes or, at long last, the sea. In the end, nature achieves a balance.

The Weasel Clan

OPPOSITE. *At home in every kind of land habitat from southern Canada into South America, the long-tailed weasel (*Mustela frenata*) is a super predator in a small and attractive package. Growing up to 24 inches long, including tail, it is normally chocolate brown with a yellowish belly, but in northern areas it turns pure white in winter— except for a black tip on its tail. Furriers call winter weasel pelts "ermine," and in medieval Europe they were reserved for the garments of royalty; 50,000 skins of the short-tailed weasel or stoat were used for the coronation of King George VI of Great Britain in 1937. Such variable beauty disguises a fierce hunter of squirrels, rabbits, snakes, frogs, insects, songbirds, and a multitude of mice and rats. Indeed, the weasel has been accused, not without cause, of killing just for fun; a weasel that finds itself in a henhouse, for instance, may slaughter dozens of chickens in a single night. One scientist called it "the most blood-thirsty of all animals," adding that "its favorite drink is warm blood sucked from the neck of its prey." And a weasel will not hesitate to attack a man who gets in its way. But this petite killer is not without its own mortal enemies: hawks, owls, and even prowling house cats.*

In the white silence of a winter woodland, a sinuous pursuit ends lethally, as with blurring speed a long-tailed weasel rockets into a fleeing cottontail and kills it with a quick thrust of needle-sharp teeth to the brain. High in a tree overlooking a wooded savanna in Africa, a honey badger, flat and brutish of face, rakes open a beehive with its hooked foreclaws and gorges on the soft pupae and the sweet contents of the combs. On the windswept high plains of the Andes, a hog-nosed skunk shuffles among the sparse vegetation, naked snout searching the ground for insects to eat. The weasels and their relatives, collectively known as the mustelid family, are among the most diverse of all the carnivores in the myriad ways they exploit their surroundings to make a living. The forests, deserts, waters, and plains of all the continents except Australia and Antarctica are inhabited by one or another of the seventy species in this group, a family characterized by a low-slung body build and by scent glands that produce a rank, even vile, odor.

The members of the weasel clan also share several other traits, notably astonishing strength for their size, tenacious ferocity, and lethal agility. It is these qualities that are responsible for the group's multifaceted success. Their fearlessness, murderous persistence, and power are legendary. The wolverine, at fifty pounds, is perhaps the strongest of all mammals for its size. Fond of carrion, it chases cougars and even bears from their kills. When it needs fresh meat, the wolverine—which since the ice ages has retreated to the northern high country and the Arctic fringes— sometimes kills moose and elk mired in snow. Deer caught in heavy snow occasionally are the prey of the North American fisher, a dozen pounds of speed and ferocity, which is also the bane of porcupines. Once it corners a porcupine, a fisher performs like a lightweight boxer. It dances and it feints, dodging the crippling blows of the porcupine's quilled tail, and darting in to repeatedly slash the porcupine's unprotected face. When the porcupine is helpless and dying, the fisher overturns it and tears open its soft underparts.

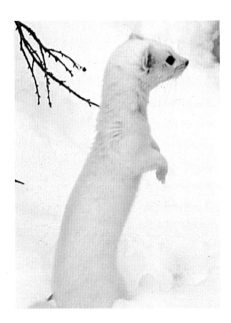  

The manner in which weasels make their kill is a chilling exercise in relentlessness. Like a slim missile homing in on a target, a long-tailed weasel will match every evasive twist and turn of a rodent or hare, as though linked to its prey by an invisible strand. Almost invariably, the chase ends with a fatal strike at the base of the victim's skull, or the neck, often delivered with blinding speed. The lithe, slender body of the weasel enables it to prowl the underground burrows of rodents with almost serpentine ease. Virtually anywhere a weasel can wedge its pointed black snout, it can take its body. Mice are tracked to the ends of their burrows, and knotholes serve as entrances to henhouses. Once inside, the weasel may slaughter as many hens as it can reach, but not because it is particularly bloodthirsty. When a weasel is confined with an abundance of prey, its highly tuned predatory responses may be difficult to shut down, and it may be unable to stop killing as long as the prey is moving.

Even trees offer no escape for the fleeing victim of a weasel, for it will go aloft after its dinner. Many members of the clan, in fact, display the same lightness of foot in the branches as on the ground. The martens do most of their hunting in the trees and subsist largely on squirrels. The tayra, a yard-long beast of the American tropics, takes to the trees to hunt arboreal anteaters and steal bananas.

Of all environments, however, the one in which the mustelids truly surpass the other carnivores is in the water. The river otters and the minks manage the weasel-like dazzling maneuvers in the water, as they swim with supple grace and swiftness after fish. They have established a virtual monopoly over the role of freshwater mammalian predator. And two of the mustelids even have followed evolutionary paths which have led to the sea, specifically the Pacific Ocean. The endangered small marine otter catches fish and other seafood where the chill waters of the Humboldt Current sweep close to the west coast of South America, from northern Peru south. Unlike its northern cousin, the sea otter, however, the marine

THIS PAGE AND OPPOSITE. *In a remarkable sequence of photographs, a long-tailed weasel sights a cottontail rabbit in the snowy mountain forests of Wyoming and launches an attack with blurring speed almost too fast for the human eye to follow. Although the rabbit is many times larger than the weasel, its size gives it no advantage over its bantam adversary, and the outcome of the pursuit is inevitable. Like a slim white missile homing on a target, the weasel stays with its chosen victim as it frantically twists and turns in the snow, finally seizing the cottontail at the base of the skull and sinking needle-sharp teeth into the brain. The hunt ended, the twelve-ounce weasel drags the three-pound rabbit off into the forest.*

otter still retains substantial links with land, for it eats its catch ashore and dens there. The endangered giant otter of South America is the longest—six feet from snout to tip of tail. Weighing hardly more than an ounce, the least weasel is the bantam among the group and, in fact, is the smallest carnivore.

Big and small, mustelids have highly developed scent glands whose secretions range in potency from slightly pungent to overpowering. The skunks, of course, are notorious for the chemical warfare they wage on their enemies. Some of their mustelid relatives, however, are just as odorous. The green secretion shot by the aptly named Malayan stink badger is supposedly potent enough to asphyxiate dogs which receive a substantial dose. The odor given off by the marbled polecat of Eurasia and Africa's zorilla is also devastating. Most of the mustelids wear some sort of contrasting blotches or stripes which warn other beasts to give them a wide berth. As a rule, the more powerful their chemical defense, the more vivid their markings.

The impact of such weapons has not been lost on humans. Witness the epithets inspired by such creatures as skunks and polecats. As a group, in fact, the mustelids probably have been associated with more unsavory human actions than any other mammals. At the same time, they have been among the most prized of creatures, valued so greatly for their furs that men have risked their lives in the wilderness to trap them. Ermine, the winter white-coated weasel, was once reserved for royalty. Marten, commercially known as sable, and mink are still reserved largely for the wealthy. What is most priceless about the members of the weasel clan, however, is their magnificent savagery, symbolic of a wild world that is rapidly becoming only a memory.

OPPOSITE. *Although they are lovely to look at, the skunks of the New World are not animals to be disturbed. An arched white-plumed tail is a fair warning to intruders that the skunk is prepared to spray—with remarkable accuracy—a foul-smelling fluid that burns the eyes and whose acrid odor persists for days. Most frequently encountered is the striped skunk* (Mephitis mephitis), *which has the distressing habit of taking up residence beneath suburban homes and summer cabins.*

TOP. *An American badger* (Taxidea taxus) *devours a rattlesnake. Using its powerful front legs, which are armed with long claws, as well as its strong jaws, a badger can dig a hole in the ground, vanish, and plug the burrow behind it in a few seconds. The badger's coarse fur once was used to make shaving brushes.*

BELOW LEFT. *A large weasel that haunts the treetops and is equipped with strong claws for climbing and a long bushy tail to keep its balance, the American marten* (Martes americana) *pursues its favorite prey, the red squirrel, through conifer forests from Newfoundland to Alaska.*

BELOW RIGHT. *An inhabitant of streams, lakes, and tidal marshes across most of North America, the mink* (Mustela vison) *is a deadly hunter of muskrats. A mink will corner one of these big aquatic rodents in its bank burrow and quickly dispatch it; or rip open a muskrat's cattail lodge, devour the young, and then claim the house as its own den.*

OVERLEAF. *Three and a half feet long, weighing perhaps fifty-five pounds, and resembling a small bear, the wolverine* (Gulo gulo) *fears no other creature. It will kill an elk or moose struggling in deep snow, drive a mountain lion away from its meal, attack a bear cub, and rob man's traplines. The wolverine roams the tundra and subarctic forests around the pole; a male wolverine requires a territory of about 1000 square miles, which overlaps the smaller territories of two or three females.*

Ancient and Unusual

OPPOSITE. *The name "pangolin" has its origin in the Malayan word* guling, *which means a long round cushion. When these timid, nocturnal ant- and termite-eaters of tropical Africa and Asia are threatened, they roll into a tight ball and erect their sharp-edged scales. Some pangolins are terrestrial, and can walk about on their hind legs using their long tails for balance. Others, like this small-scaled tree pangolin of Africa with its baby (*Manis tricuspis*), are arboreal and their tails are prehensile. The armored tails also can be wielded as a wicked mace.*

When the platypus was first brought to the attention of European scientists almost two centuries ago, in the form of a skin, they considered it a fraud. Their error can be excused, for the platypus is so bizarre that even today it is difficult to believe such a creature exists and is, indeed, rather common in some of the lakes, ponds, and streams of eastern Australia and Tasmania. The platypus has a look of ultimate incongruity. Its broadened snout superficially resembles the bill of a duck. Its tail is flattened like a beaver's, and its webbed feet approximate those of an otter. The hind feet of the male, moreover, carry spurs which, totally out of character for a mammal, are venomous. The female, in an even more astonishing departure from the mammalian norm, lays eggs, reptilian in aspect.

Other oddities include the tree sloths of tropical America, which live a slow-motion existence hanging upside down and sometimes appear green in color because of the algae growing on their hair. The sloths' relatives, the armadillos, and other armored creatures also belong to the group. So do the echidnas—the only other living egg-laying mammals besides the platypus—and the frantic, furious shrews.

Actually, these and the others grouped here are only strange from a human perspective. Their queer appendages and odd behavior are merely manifestations of the many ways in which animals have adapted to varying modes of life. The odd combination of organs in the platypus, for instance, superbly equips it for feeding along the muddy bottoms of the streams and lakes whose banks hold its burrows. The fleshy tentacles that tip the snout of the American star-nosed mole serve a similar purpose when the little creature forages along the bottom of streams and ponds, in a dramatic demonstration of how moles can swim as well as burrow. Underground, even more than underwater, the moles also rely on their tactile, naked snouts to feel for food. Their remarkable sense of touch compensates for their extremely poor eyesight and even, in the case of species such as the eastern American mole, the lack of external eyes.

LEFT ABOVE AND BELOW. *The North American porcupine* (Erethizon dorsatum), *which may reach a weight of forty pounds, has two easily recognized forms. The spines of the porcupine of western forests, from Alaska to New Mexico, are tipped with yellow and surrounded by long fuzzy hairs; those of its eastern counterpart are tipped with black.*

CENTER TOP. *The prehensile-tailed porcupines* (Coendou sp.) *of Central and South American tropical forests vary in color from almost white to almost black. They are nocturnal and arboreal, and their tails lack spines and are naked on top for curling under rather than over tree branches.*

Parallel adaptations for coping with the same sort of life situations link many of the otherwise unrelated animals in the assemblage described here. Dietary reliance upon tropical ants and termites, which must be dug from nests as hard as concrete, has shaped several other creatures from separate evolutionary lines in an equally unusual manner. The anteaters of the American tropics, the pangolins of Africa and southern Asia, the aardvark of Africa, and even the little echidnas of Australia and New Guinea all have large, powerful claws for digging, few or even no teeth, tubular snouts, and tongues of snakelike proportions, sticky with modified saliva, for plucking up ants and termites. The evolutionary paths taken by the pangolins and the anteaters in their respective hemispheres converge even more dramatically in some of their smaller

72

RIGHT. *Like the platypus, the echidnas or spiny anteaters of New Guinea and Australia are egg-laying mammals, the female incubating her single leathery-shelled egg in a pocket that develops on her belly during the breeding season. The short-nosed spiny anteater (Tachyglossus aculeatus) has only one enemy—aboriginal man, who likes to eat its ant-scented meat.*

CENTER BOTTOM. *Few predators are able to attack a Western European hedgehog (Erinaceus europaeus) successfully, for it buries its vulnerable head, belly, and legs in an impenetrable ball of spines. The spines also cushion the impact when the hedgehog falls or drops from a tree.*

representatives which, unlike the larger types, have taken to the trees. The tamandua and the squirrel-sized silky anteater and two species of African tree pangolins have prehensile tails, which provide an extra holdfast while they attack the nests of arboreal ants and termites.

Digging also furnishes some of the creatures that live on termites and ants a means of escaping from danger. The echidnas can vanish in a twinkling, as though swallowed by the earth. The echidna wedges itself into the ground not only with its powerful feet but with its coat of spines. If for some reason it cannot burrow, it rolls itself into a ball, in effect a living pincushion. Most of the armored creatures that can be classed as unusual opt for similar defenses if in trouble. The pangolin, which is covered with scales of modified hair, as if in imitation of a pine cone, locks itself into a ball impossible to unravel. The hairy armadillo and the pichi armadillo anchor themselves in their burrows with the edges of their body armor, which really is skin-covered bony plates. If caught in the open the hairy armadillo will hunker down under its armor, which touches the ground at its lower edges.

Some of the porcupines, which share with the echidnas and hedgehogs hairs that have taken the form of spines, use their quills aggressively when attacked by flesh eaters. The Old World porcupines, which can reach a size of sixty pounds, sometimes bristle their quills and dash into an attacker. The North American porcupine swings its quilled tail like a spiked club. The quills of porcupines, needle sharp, detach when their points penetrate an enemy, working their way deep into the flesh, sometimes with fatal results.

Extremes always are bizarre, at either end of the scale, which is one reason why the shrews, some of the smallest of living mammals, must be counted among the unusual. As is the case with some other very small mammals, shrews must consume tremendous amounts of food to fill their

energy needs, and must refuel with worms, insects, and even other small mammals every few hours. Some of the shrews rely not only upon the legendary ferocity of their attack to down relatively large prey, but also upon a weapon otherwise virtually unknown in mammals—a venomous bite. The American short-tailed shrew has enough venom in its salivary glands to kill 200 mice.

The shrews, moles, hedgehogs, and the other insectivores—notably the tenrecs of Madagascar—are among the more primitive of the placental mammals. The first placental mammals, appearing long before the Age of Reptiles ended, may have resembled tenrecs, and perhaps shrews. But the links the insectivores have with the past pale before the credentials of the monotremes, whose living representatives are the platypus and the echidnas. Although mammals, they retain so many reptilian features that it is certain they arose long before either the marsupials or the higher mammals and may represent a separate crossing of the mammal-reptile line. This is evidenced not only by the fact that, of all living mammals, only they lay eggs, but also by internal features, such as bone structure, and the reptilian sprawl of their legs. They are living reminders of our scaly, cold-blooded past.

The Hunters: Dogs

Creeping low to the ground, its tail outstretched, its belly almost brushing the earth, the red fox stalks a cottontail. Slowly, sharp nose pointed in the rabbit's direction, it inches imperceptibly toward its prey. A dozen feet away it halts, still concealed by the undergrowth. Its body tenses, muscles bunch, and it explodes out of hiding, darting for its prey, which spurts away, with the fox in swift, silent pursuit.

The dog family consists of hunters generally built for the chase, although some members are sufficiently sly to catch prey by stealth. A few, generally only the smaller members of the group, are solitary hunters. The agile, intelligent red fox prowls the land alone, as silently as a blown leaf, ready to run down a rabbit if necessary, but also eager to pounce upon a mouse that has stirred in the grass. In its hunting methods, it sometimes behaves more like a cat than a dog. The gray fox of North America is also a lone hunter. Nightly, it follows the same route, a twisted, winding course over the countryside as it casts about for small rodents. Similarly, the coyote is prone to patrolling its territory over a regular hunting trail, night after night, even year after year. Yet for the coyote the hunt can also be a family affair, which is why coyotes, seldom exceeding thirty pounds, can sometimes kill prey that is bigger, stronger, and faster than they, and it is this aspect of their behavior that so strongly characterizes the group. The members of a coyote family will take turns running a pronghorn antelope in a circle until it falls from exhaustion, whereupon all the coyotes move in for the kill.

At their most devastating, the canine hunters work as highly organized, efficient teams, ranging from two to a dozen or more members. Deep-chested, lean, and long of leg, the canine hunters are typified by their seemingly ruthless and relentless hunts. Actually, they employ only the degree of violence necessary to make a kill. The evolution of team tactics among them has been accompanied by the growth of social organizations that are so sophisticated and complex they rival those of the most advanced primates. The technique of

OPPOSITE. *Largest of all wild dogs, a wolf (Canis lupus) may stand thirty inches at the shoulders and weigh 150 pounds and is capable of bringing down prey as big as musk-oxen and caribou.*

hunting as a group is most highly developed among the wolves, African hunting dogs, and the dholes of Asia, all now endangered.

These creatures form hunting packs that operate with superb coordination, and regularly kill animals which easily could repel the attack of a single one of their number. In addition to their exceptional organization and coordination as hunting packs, canine hunters also succeed by endurance. In large packs, one group of hunters may take over the lead as another group tires, or as the prey zig-zags to escape. Wolf packs may split up to separate a cow moose from her calf. A few members of the pack will drive the cow, harrying her so that gradually they split her from the calf, pressing her farther and farther from her offspring, while the remainder of the pack pursue the calf.

Dholes hunt primarily by scent, an advantage in the thick cover they generally inhabit. They may chase the prey all together, or they may split

ABOVE. *A pack of wolves pursues a moose— unsuccessfully this time—in the deep snows of Isle Royale National Park, in Michigan. The wolves of this forty-mile-long wilderness preserve in Lake Superior are equally famous in research circles. Breeding wolves first reached Isle Royale in the late 1940s, crossing eighteen miles of ice from the Ontario shore. Their unexpected arrival was nature's answer to a dilemma—a population of moose that, in the absence of any predator, had exploded and severely overbrowsed the forest. Today, two dozen wolves live on Isle Royale in careful balance with a moose herd that in midwinter averages a thousand animals. Severely endangered in the wild, there are probably only 35 wolves left in Michigan and Wisconsin combined.*

80

up, with some members of the pack waiting on the edge of the forest for the prey to be flushed into the open. Wolves and African hunting dogs, which often live in the open, hunt largely by eye, but if they are seeking prey in the forest or thick bush, they also nose about in an effort to pinpoint the location of their victim. Large targets, such as an adult antelope, may stand their ground and fight, and more often than is generally believed, drive off their tormentors. But once the victim chooses to flee, the advantage is with the pack, which strings out in pursuit, sometimes running in relays, until exhaustion forces the hunted creature to stop.

Once the quarry of the pack has been brought to bay, the tactics used by all of the wild dogs are the same. If the prey is small, it is immediately overwhelmed. Large victims are encircled by dancing, darting forms, trying from every direction for a telling bite. Wolves and African hunting

THIS PAGE AND OPPOSITE. *African wild dogs* (Lycaon pictus) *are famous among animal behaviorists for their highly organized social life. Groups of anywhere from a half-dozen to thirty wild dogs live as a close-knit pack, within which food and pup-rearing responsibilities are shared. While some dogs hunt, pursuing wildebeests, warthogs, gazelles, and zebras across the savanna at speeds reaching 30 miles an hour, another member of the pack stands guard at the den—usually an old aardvark hole—where the litter of up to sixteen pups is hidden. When the hunters return, they regurgitate partly digested meat to feed the nursing female, young, and aged members of the pack.*

OPPOSITE. *The gray fox* (Urocyon cinereoargenteus) *of North America to Venezuela has remarkable habits for a member of the dog family: it climbs trees and likes to eat ripe fruit and grain.*

RIGHT. *Falling snow dusts the thick pelt of a red fox* (Vulpes vulpes) *sleeping off a heavy meal. On Isle Royale in winter, scavenging foxes are a principal beneficiary of moose kills by the wolf pack.*

OVERLEAF. *Speedster of the eastern and southern African woodlands, the black-backed jackal* (Canis mesomelas) *can run 40 miles an hour in pursuit of gazelles, although fruit and rodents form the bulk of its diet.*

dogs customarily try for a grip on the snout of the victim. When one of the pack has managed to hold fast, the rest attack the quarry from the rear, trying to get it to the ground.

As might be surmised, to cooperate so smoothly, packs must be highly structured and joined by strong communal ties. The pack is, then, a form of extended-family unit, which serves not only to provide food but to protect as well. Youngsters growing up within the pack benefit from the ties that hold it together. Wolves, hunting dogs, and dholes swallow chunks of flesh at the kill, then return to the young and regurgitate it for them to eat.

The size of a pack varies from a few to more than two dozen members, but to remain a cohesive unit, it needs local prey large enough to fill all the stomachs. Groups of less than a few prime adults are at a tremendous disadvantage, not only in dispatching large prey, but also in defending the kill from other carnivores. Where food is abundant, and large prey abounds, the size of the pack can increase without some of its members going hungry after a kill. But if a pack is so large that even successful hunts leave many members still famished, it will break down into smaller units, perhaps only temporarily for purposes of hunting, but in some cases permanently into two or more new packs.

Thus, the hunting pack, as formed by wild canines, is a means of exploiting food that would seldom if ever be available, without the strength that comes from unity.

The Hunters: Cats

Its passage heralded by the sharp yaps of the little muntjacs, or barking deer, a tiger walks the land. Moving fluidly, the massive muscles in its shoulders undulating to match its strides, it pads through a green tongue of woodland below a sunlit, grassy hillside. At the margin of the trees, the tiger pauses. The great, ruffed head turns slowly. The eyes, with chilling assurance, survey the landscape. Scattered in knots on the verdant slope ahead are sambar deer. They are feeding, their dark bodies gilded by the sun of the late afternoon. As the tiger scans the hillside, a wave of perturbation sweeps over the little clusters of deer. Heads are raised. Ears twitch. Nostrils quiver wetly, inquisitively, testing the soft breeze. The deer sense that, in the peace of the declining day, death has arrived.

The cats are many in species, diverse in size, but alike in mien and in that, from the largest, the 700-pound tiger of Siberian snows, to the dainty margay of South America, they are all killers. They live by killing, and the more efficiently they do it, the better the chances that their progeny will survive.

Adaptation to this end has conferred a terrible majesty upon some of them, especially the larger ones. It has made all of them sleek and silent, stealthy and supple, so that even the smallest seem to possess both an inscrutable cunning and vast dignity. It has armed them with muscles that can move fluidly but with sledgehammer power, with fearsome teeth and hooked claws that can either hold a victim fast or rake the life from it. The cats need all of these advantages, for they face the unending task of killing enough prey to survive, and must surmount enormous obstacles to accomplish it.

Concealment, then a sudden bound or explosive rush, is favored by most of the feline hunters, but within the overall pattern the hunt takes many forms. A stealthy, solitary stalk is the way of most cats, both the smaller ones, such as the African wild cat, and their larger relatives. The tiger creeps to within a few yards of the victim, then launches its attack from the rear or the flank, fastening its claws into the body of the prey

OPPOSITE AND OVERLEAF. *The cheetah* (Acinonyx jubatus) *is capable of incredible speed—nearly 70 miles an hour—but only in short bursts. If it fails to bring down its carefully selected target within about 600 yards, the pursuit is given up, for by then the cat is totally exhausted. Cheetahs prey most often on medium-sized antelopes, but they can bring down an animal as large as a young wildebeest, killing with a throat bite—then eating meat off the thighs, forelegs, and ribcage, before eating the liver, kidneys, and heart.*

89

LEFT. *Named for the German naturalist Peter Simon Pallas, who was noted for his scientific explorations of Russia and Siberia in the eighteenth century, Pallas's cat (Otocolobus manul) has small ears and long fur on its flanks, belly, and tail—adaptations for life in the cold, snowy steppes of central Asia.*

RIGHT. *Cautiously stalking the dry grasslands, savannas, and bush country of Africa and southern Asia, the caracal (Felis caracal caracal) preys on rodents, hares, ostriches, and small antelopes. It will leap into a low-flying flock of birds to bring down several at a time. This rare desert relative of the lynx once was trained to hunt game for man.*

LEFT. *Enemy of snakes in the tropical American rain forests, an ocelot (Leopardus pardalis) can dispatch even a boa constrictor. Male and female ocelots hunt in cooperative fashion, meowing to one another like house cats, and they share in rearing the young.*

RIGHT. *Hunter of northern forests around the world, the lynx (Lynx canadensis) has huge, hairy feet that enable it to travel over deep snow without sinking. In Canada, the life of the lynx is inexorably tied to the snowshoe hare, it chief prey; the hare population is cyclic, and when it plunges every seven years, lynx numbers likewise suffer a severe decrease.*

LEFT. *The cougar (Puma concolor) once stalked the New World wilderness from the Atlantic to the Pacific, from northern Canada almost to the tip of South America. Hunted as a game trophy, persecuted as a killer of livestock, intolerant of civilization, the cougar has vanished from most of its historic haunts, and is endangered. Weighing 200 pounds, it can easily bring down a large deer and lug the carcass back to its den.*

RIGHT. *Big, round ears that almost touch identify the serval (Felis serval) of Africa's woodland savannas. Resembling a scaled-down cheetah, the serval has long, slender forelegs that it uses to probe rocky crevices and dens in search of rodents.*

while it bites the neck. The hunt sometimes takes the shape of a spectacular acrobatic performance, like the leaps of the slender, long-legged serval of Africa. With blinding speed, it bounds through the high savanna grasses, flushing birds, and springing after them to claw them out of the air six feet above the ground.

Whatever the style of the hunt, however, success depends upon the ability to work close enough to the prey in secret so it can be brought down in a single, decisive maneuver. The nature of the maneuver depends upon the particular physical assets of the cat that performs it. The cougar of the Americas is fast enough to overtake a deer on a course of a hundred yards or so. Usually, however, the conditions under which the cougar hunts are far from ideal, so it tries to get within a few yards where it can strike like an uncoiled steel spring, hurtling into its victim and even bowling it over. The caracal, a sand-colored lynx of Africa and Asia, relies on its superior ability to ambush its prey. For these and the other cats, the hunt is almost always a solitary affair, except when mothers are teaching their young the skills of the killer. A major exception to the rule, however, is the lion, most social of all the cats, the only one to live in large family groups, and as often as not a team hunter. Lions, or more precisely lionesses, regularly hunt as a group, with some members of the pride driving prey into the jaws of the others.

The strength of the cats, relative to size, is awesome. A leopard, which seldom weighs more than a man, commonly hauls prey almost as heavy as itself into a tree and stows it in the branches for a later meal. Cougars, about the weight of leopards, have dragged off horses many times heavier than themselves. Buffalo, gaur, wild boar, oryx, moose, caribou, elk—all but the very largest herbivores regularly fall prey to the bigger cats. The prey is often quite varied, however, proof of the adaptability of the group. Caimans in the water and monkeys in the trees furnish meals for the stocky, powerful jaguar, whose range extends from the tropics into the southwestern United States. Tigers sometimes rove the mangrove swamps at seaside in search of fish and even turtles. Lions occasionally pounce upon rats, in imitation of their smaller, domestic relatives.

While most cats are adaptable predators, some are so specialized that they possess anatomical features that uniquely equip them to hunt a certain prey in a specific habitat. The Canadian lynx, for example, with its large snowshoe feet, preys mainly upon the big varying hare, or "snowshoe rabbit," which itself has large furry feet for locomotion over the crusted snow.

The effects of specialization also are revealed in the body of the cheetah, which relies mainly upon small, fleet gazelles as prey. The cheetah, unlike the other cats, is built not so much for stealth as for speed. Its conformation in some ways approaches that of the wild dogs, which run down their prey rather than surprise it. This large, spotted cat has exceptionally long legs, and its claws, like those of the dogs, are heavy and

LEFT AND RIGHT OVERLEAF. *Of eight races of tigers living in the 19th century, the Javan, Balinese, and Caspian tigers are extinct; the remainder will probably be extinct by 1999. Of some races, less than a hundred animals may survive. Most numerous, if three or four thousand can be considered numerous, is the Indian tiger* (Panthera tigris tigris), *but it is presently being poached and its habitat destroyed. This solitary hunter is the largest cat on earth; a male may stand three feet at the shoulders, measure thirteen feet in length including its tail, and weigh 575 pounds. Few animals are beyond the tiger's great strength—baby elephants and rhinos, are taken, as are gaurs and water buffalos—and a tiger may claim a kill from a leopard. Its appetite is voracious: a healthy tiger requires three tons of meat a year, the equivalent of thirty domestic cattle or seventy axis deer. But its meals do not come easy. To make a kill, a tiger must stalk to within a few feet of the victim, then bring it down with a final lunge. If it misses, the cat may chase the prey a hundred yards or so, but with little chance of catching it. Thus the tiger often augments its diet with more easily obtained fish, frogs, turtles, rodents, even locusts. Tigers readily take to water, swimming with ease across swift rivers, large lakes, or bays.*

THIS PAGE AND OPPOSITE. *Lions* (Panthera leo) *are famous for the gentle and affectionate family life in a pride that may include two or three males, ten lionesses, and their young of varying ages. Male lions tolerate the rough romping and food stealing of the cubs, but there is a lot of noisy squabbling among adults over kills, and males often wrest food from their mates. After a meal, however, calm prevails. Lion cubs — two to four to a litter — weigh about three pounds at birth. They are weaned in three to six months and immediately begin taking hunting lessons from their mother. Young males must leave the pride at the age of three and a half years, but lionesses often remain for their entire lives. Wildebeests, zebras, and the ubiquitous little Thomson's gazelles are the usual prey of a pride.*

OVERLEAF. *Prey of the bobcat* (Lynx rufus) *runs the gamut from little deer mice to adult deer. Growing up to sixty-six pounds of muscle and sinew, the bobcat — its trademark is its tail, which appears to have been bobbed — hunts the forests, swamps, and deserts of North America from coast to coast, and from the Canadian border deep into Mexico. It exists surprisingly close to towns and cities, but humans are rarely aware of its presence except during the mating season, late in the winter, when the bobcat rends the nighttime silence with frightening squalls and yowls. Its beautiful pelt has come into great demand and this has triggered heavy trapping pressure.*

blunt. The claws of the cheetah are for traction during running, not for grasping prey. When it hunts, it relies on its keen eyes and capacity for a sudden burst of speed — up to 70 miles an hour — which no other creature on four legs can match over a short distance. The only hope of the cheetah's prey is to twist and turn until the fleet cat tires and, sensing its limitations, gives up the chase. Often, evasive tactics are successful, and the cheetah is left panting and hungry. But when the hunt of the cheetah goes in its favor, the pursuit ends in a roil of dust and a welling of blood. It is a stark reminder that the purpose of the hunting beast is the cessation of life, but for a reason — so that other life can continue. It is symbolic of the endless cycle of death and renewal that is nature.

Big Bears
and Their Kin

OPPOSITE. *Although the giant panda (Ailuropoda melanoleuca) is a symbol of wildlife conservation around the world, its life in the mountain forests of China remains largely a mystery more than a century after its discovery. Scientists know that the giant panda eats copious amounts of bamboo shoots, a food with low nutritional value, and that its striking black-and-white coloration is an effective camouflage as the 300-pound animal sits on its haunches high in a tree. One of the rarest mammals in the world, there are only a few hundred giant pandas left in the wild, and it is considered a national treasure by the Chinese, who call it* beishiung-chin, *meaning "white bear." Taxonomists still debate the giant panda's true relationships, some saying it is closer to the bears than to raccoons. But most recently, the giant panda and the red panda have been placed within the bear family.*

The hulking form shambles to the water's edge, wades in, and plops down on its rump. Sitting in a stream with the water up to its chest, an Alaskan brown bear seems to be giving an impression of a big, hairy man enjoying a bath. There is much about the bears, in fact, that encourages an anthropomorphism, for in many of their mannerisms, including even their style of walking, with the entire underpart of the foot touching the ground, they seem to caricature humans. It is, however, an illusion that is quickly dispelled when a bear is aroused to battle. Half-ton bodies no longer shuffle, but move explosively, almost lithely, with furious power. Piggy snouts quiver wetly and lips are drawn back to reveal huge canine fangs, yellowed and wickedly curved. Any anthropomorphic resemblances vanish in a scene of immense bestiality.

Yet the bears similarity to humans crops up again and again. An American black bear stands up to beg for handouts in a national park. A polar bear plunges with apparent joy from an ice cliff into the sea. The same sort of behavior is carried on by certain members of another family of creatures, related to the bears and typified by the raccoon. In the raccoon's case, it is the creature's appealing manner and especially the use of its forepaw which contribute most to the fancy that it is really a little round man in a fur suit. Other than primates, few creatures have digits which so closely simulate human fingers in form and function. The resemblance was not lost upon the Algonquin Indians. The name "raccoon" comes from the Algonquian word *aroughcoune*, which means "he who scratches with his hands." The "hands" of the raccoon are a marvel. It and its South American cousin, the crab-eating raccoon, have a wonderfully delicate touch, a sense so highly developed that they rely on it almost exclusively when dabbling in the shallows for crustaceans, fish, frogs, and other food.

Highly adaptable to human presence, the raccoon manages to exist even in cities, and thrives in suburbs, where the contents of backyard garbage cans provide an endless supply of food. Encountered while on

101

a nocturnal foray into the trash can, a raccoon may pause with a purloined tidbit raised halfway to its mouth, and stare quizzically at the intruder as if to ask why it has been disturbed at its dining. At such times it can be a charming animal. If cornered by dogs, however, the raccoon displays another facet to its nature. It is transformed from a seemingly amiable clown into a ball of fighting fury. Cunning and tenacious, a raccoon is more than a match for a dog of its size.

The raids by raccoons on garbage cans testify to the omnivorous diet of these creatures, a trait shared by other members of its family and most bears. Coatis, ranging in troops of from a few to dozens of animals, poke their long snouts into virtually every crack and cranny in their path, eating everything from fruit to small mammals.

Among the bears, the most specialized in terms of eating habits is the polar bear, for it spends most of its life on the ice or at sea, away from vegetation save an occasional strand of seaweed. The great white bear

ABOVE. *Stalking the pack ice and frigid waters around the North Pole in search of seals and walruses, the polar bear (Ursus maritimus) is one of the great nomads of the mammal kingdom. It spends most of its life at sea, often floating hundreds of miles from land on great ice floes. A powerful swimmer, the polar bear has front paws that are partially webbed, and a water-repellent coat that keeps the animal warm even after hours in the water. Polar bears come ashore only occasionally, varying their diet with tundra berries or hunting down a caribou or musk-ox. In winter, females make a snow den on land to give birth to their cubs, which number from one to three.*

subsists almost entirely on flesh, mostly of seals, and has even been known to stalk humans on the ice in much the same way it hunts pinnipeds.

The Asiatic black bear, a 300-pound creature with a reputation for aggressiveness, will occasionally attack and kill cattle and sheep. So at times will the big brown bears, including the grizzly of North America. Generally, however, they prey on creatures no larger than rodents.

The Alaskan browns—some of which weigh more than 1600 pounds, stand almost a dozen feet high, and are the largest living land carnivores—gather at streams where salmon spawn. Shaggy coats dripping, the bears dash and plunge about in the foaming water, grabbing and snapping after the pink-fleshed fish.

The spectacled bear of South America and the little Malayan sun bear, obtain much of their food from the trees. The spectacled bear, so called because of the light markings that ring its eyes, hauls its 300-pound body aloft to a true nest, but forages much on the ground for palm stalks, new leaves, and seeds. The sun bear—the only bear smaller than an average human being—lives in a tree nest and eats fruit and the soft young growth of coconut palms. The raccoons and their relatives are even more adept in the branches. Raccoons often nest in tree hollows and take refuge in the trees when pursued by dogs and hunters. Two other members of the family, the olingo and the kinkajou, are the equal of monkeys in the trees. They are night rovers, wide of eye, and quietly search the forest canopy for the fruit they relish above all else.

Looking like a rust-colored raccoon, but possibly more closely related to the bears, the lesser panda of southwestern China and bordering lands further demonstrates arboreal proclivities. The little red panda sleeps in the trees by day, its brushy tail wrapped around its head, and although it generally forages on the ground, it uses the trees as a refuge and tree hollows as dens. Even the giant panda, as much a model for children's dolls and figurines as the "teddy bear" koala of Australia, will climb into the trees if pursued, although it can weigh upward of 300 pounds. Few mammals have caused so much difficulty for those people whose job it is to classify the members of the animal kingdom. The giant panda, now endangered, shares characteristics with both bears and raccoons, but recent morphological and molecular studies suggest it belongs in the bear family. The black-and-white panda has been a problem for the classifiers for only a century or so, because Western science did not know of the creature until the late 1860s. It was then that Jean Pierre Armand David, a Roman Catholic priest and naturalist, ventured into the rugged bamboo-covered territory of western China and Tibet and in all likelihood became the first European to see the creature. For the peoples of the West, David had found a new and curious animal. For the classifiers, he had created a problem that has taken more than one hundred years to resolve.

OPPOSITE AND OVERLEAF. *The grizzly or brown bear* (Ursus arctos) *has been the center of many controversies ever since white man first intruded into its domain in the North American West. Most have been serious matters of survival for both bear and man. Not so the long-running battle over its name —or names. As one noted zoologist wrote, "Probably no other piece of research has brought dignified mammalogists nearer to name-calling and nose-punching than the question of correctly classifying the grizzly bear." The argument is between the "lumpers" and "splitters" in the taxonomic fraternity, which relies heavily on the shape of mammals' skulls and teeth in determining their classification. And the problem is the great variation in skulls and teeth among these big carnivores. Thus one scientist, a splitter in the extreme, decided there were eighty-four different species and subspecies of grizzly and brown bears in North America, and he claimed five distinct species could be found on one Alaskan island only a hundred miles long! Today, however, the lumpers rule. They tell us only a single species of brown bear is found across the entire Northern Hemisphere. Smallest of the local races is the 200-pound Syrian bear; largest of all is the Kodiak bear of coastal Alaska, a giant that stands nine feet tall on its hind legs and weighs 1600 pounds. All have the same ominous appearance—a hollowed-out face and a big hump between the shoulders. In North America, the term "grizzly" was first applied to the bears of the Rocky Mountain wilderness and "brown bear" to those that haunt the Alaska coast, feeding on grass, berries, and other vegetable matter much of the year but growing fat in midsummer on salmon.*

LEFT. *A group of lesser pandas* (Ailurus fulgens), *long-tailed Asian members of a family long thought to be related to both bears and raccoons. The lesser panda frequents the mountain forests and bamboo thickets on the south-facing slopes of the Himalayas, from Nepal to Burma and the Chinese provinces of Yunnan and Szechwan. It too feeds extensively on bamboo, grasping the shoots with prehensile thumbs and chewing the tough fiber with powerful jaws and large teeth. But unlike the giant panda, it is not strictly vegetarian, for it eats nestling birds, eggs, rodents, and insects captured on its nocturnal ventures.*

The Deer Tribe

Lying in the snows of January, an antler discarded by a whitetail buck affirms the continuity of nature, the marvelous cycle of life that progresses unbroken through the endless round of seasons. Crusted with ice, perhaps, or gnawed by rodents, the jettisoned tree of bone on the woodland floor promises new life to come from old. Antlers are the peculiar property of the deer family, half a hundred species of generally graceful cud chewers native to the Americas, Eurasia, some large Far Eastern islands, and northwestern Africa, and widely introduced beyond those areas. Although sometimes used in defense against predators, the primary role of antlers is for intimidation of rivals during mating, ultimately expediting the inheritance by the young of genes rich in survival value.

The sexual import of antlers is signified by the fact that they are mostly carried only by the males and employed in bruising tournaments to gain dominance and the right to mate with females. There are some exceptions to the all-male rule. Both sexes of the Eurasian reindeer and its North American counterpart, the caribou, carry antlers. But antlers are entirely missing from either sex of the Chinese water deer and its distant cousin—not a true deer—the small musk deer. Instead, they have sharp canine tusks in the upper jaw. Oddities today, they may resemble the creatures from which the deer tribe arose, for the ancestors of the deer showed no signs of antlers.

During the past 25 million years or so, however, antlers have appeared and evolved into myriad sizes and configurations. Those of the foot-high pudus of South America are slender, finger-length spikes. But the 1800-pound North American moose carries massive, palmate antlers that have a spread of more than six feet.

Changes in the antlers as they bud, grow, and eventually deteriorate mirror changes in the life of the deer as they move through their yearly reproductive cycle. Shedding of the antlers signals that mating is past, that males may join one another or on occasion even mix with the females without conflict or sexual involvement. The Eurasian roe deer mates in

summer and sheds in autumn. The Père David's deer of China, extinct as a wild animal for centuries but preserved in zoos, follows a similar cycle. The American whitetail, which ranges in size from more than 300 pounds in the North to a 50-pound race of midgets in the Florida Keys, mates in autumn and is without its antlers by midwinter.

For most deer, the rutting season opens just as the antlers become gleaming hard. Their maturation heralds the beginning of competition between the males, a contest that may be waged at levels of which we are oblivious. The antlers almost certainly express the dominance of the fittest males in more subtle ways. A splendid set of antlers unquestionably advertises the vitality of its owner, and indeed, the growing of antlers is intimately linked to the production of the male hormone testosterone. A stag that is neutered while it is immature, and thus deprived of testosterone, never produces antlers. A spayed female injected with it develops a rudimentary set of antlers.

Mature antler is bone which has grown rapidly out of the skull and then died. No other bone grows so profusely after birth. While growing, the antler is linked internally to the blood supply of the skull. As the bone hardens, the linkage is carried out through vessels in the velvet, the tender skin over the growing antler. Eventually, as hormones ebb and flow in the body, the blood supply dwindles, and the velvet shrivels, frays, and is rubbed off on trees and other objects.

When their antlers are polished and ready, the males, which generally have lived by themselves for several months, roam in search of females. Most male deer announce their readiness to mate—and to do battle—with challenging calls that blast over the landscape. The moose emits a raspy roar. The North American mule deer gives out loud grunts. The graceful fallow deer, introduced to Europe from the Middle East as early as classical times, coughs.

The red deer, fabled stag of medieval legend and lore, and of the golden artwork of the Scythians, challenges with a harsh, grating bellow that leaves little doubt it means business. The bugle of the elk is one of the most thrilling sounds in the animal kingdom. The mere bugle of a big bull can send a rival fleeing.

There comes a time, however, when males of equivalent size and strength clash. Elk and moose pairs come together with head-shattering clashes. Sometimes one is killed or injured, but usually the weaker backs off. The greatest danger to the combatants is that the antlers will lock, leaving them to slow, grim death by starvation.

Male deer that triumph in mating battles often gather large harems about them. Caribou and reindeer bulls may have up to forty cows, some with their young. Mule deer are somewhat lackadaisical, and gather only three or four females, which are allowed to wander off. Moose often remain with one cow, but also sometimes spread their attention among several. Once mating is complete, male deer leave the females. Often the males remain in bachelor herds until the next rut approaches, but sometimes, especially in winter, deer will form loose herds of both sexes.

With the end of breeding, the antler loses its purpose. Ironically, it is cast off because it starts to grow again. The spurt of new growth occurs on the frontal bones of the skull, in the bony platform from which the antler arose. The antler, however, is dead, and cannot respond to growth, so the force of new cells piling up below pushes it up and away from the skull, until it is so loosely joined that a casual blow, or even a vigorous shake of the head, will dislodge it. Fallen to the ground, the antler is a silent message declaring that nature regenerates itself even as it dies.

OPPOSITE. *Late-afternoon sun highlights the budding, velvet-covered antlers and outside ears of a mule deer (Odocoileus hemionus), the deer of mountains and deserts of western North America. Mule deer are noted for the strange way they run in flight, bounding in four-foot-high leaps, looking backward each time to check on their pursuers. In some areas, local people call it the jumping deer. Mule deer are plagued in summer with ticks—thousands of them on a single animal—and, like the oxpeckers that accompany the wild buffalo of Africa, magpies and jays will perch on a deer's back and pluck off the pests. Occasionally one deer will chew at the parasites on another deer. Black bears and the rare grizzly prey heavily on mule deer fawns, and coyotes will try to bring down an adult, but more often than not it will be routed or killed by flailing hooves. The mule deer's big eyes give it superb vision in the dim light of dawn and dusk.*

OVERLEAF. *A flashing white "flag" disappearing into the dense forest is often a hiker's only clue that he has startled a white-tailed deer (Odocoileus virginianus) into flight. The large, waving tail is probably an alarm signal that also aids group members in staying together during flight.*

SECOND OVERLEAF. *It is autumn on the Alaska tundra, and shreds of velvet hang from the tender, blood-red antlers of a bull caribou (Rangifer tarandus). The caribou herds have formed up for the migration to their winter range, and a large bull like this will have stored up fifty pounds of fat on its back and rump in preparation for the forthcoming battles of the rutting season. Scraped clean and polished against willows and spruce, the antlers will be put to hard use before they are shed as the heavy snows fall.*

Grazing Herds

OPPOSITE. *The national symbol of South Africa, the springbuck (*Antidorcas marsupialis*) is named for the peculiar way it jumps, or stots, when excited. Holding its legs stiff and its hooves together, the springbuck bounces vertically like a child on a pogo stick, a pouch of white hairs opening on its arched back and flashing at the peak of its ten-foot leaps. One "pronking" springbuck is likely to start an entire herd bouncing. Herds of hundreds of thousands of springbucks once migrated across the dry grasslands, but they were decimated late in the nineteenth century by colonists attempting to protect their crops and by a great rinderpest epidemic in 1896.*

Hours before the fall of night, the savanna has been darkened, not by shadows but by the slate-colored forms of the wildebeest, immense herds of them arriving from the dry lands to the south. Leaving the dusty expanses of the Serengeti Plain to the gazelles and ostriches, the wildebeest have made their annual flight from drought. When night finally does cloak the landscape, the air is heavy with the presence of the herds, with a great but muffled stirring of bodies, punctuated by breathy snorts and occasional grunts.

The migration of the Serengeti wildebeest echoes the mass movements of the enormous herds of hoofed herbivores that once occurred throughout the vast plains of Africa, Eurasia, and North America. These open grasslands have been the home of multitudes of grazing creatures, chiefly antelopes, wild cattle, and their relatives. Some animals, such as the European bison and the African buffalo, live in the forests, where they graze grass in open glades or along river courses. But for millennia the vast herds have inhabited plains of far horizons.

For the wildebeest—and until a century ago for the American bison—one of the patterns of life is a seasonal change in range, accomplished by a migratory trek. But for all the horned herds, the cycle of nature's year causes changes that shape their lives even more profoundly than a seasonal shift of scene. Entire animal societies, unshakably stable part of the year, break down and are restructured. The behavior of individuals may change so drastically that they act like entirely new forms of animals. For instance, the male Grant's gazelle or the hartebeest that has lived peaceably with others of its sex for months suddenly becomes solitary and cantankerous. Bull African buffalos which lived on the fringes of the herd become more gregarious. The timing of such changes of pattern is geared to the survival of the species and of individuals. Correlated to conditions in the environment, the timetable promotes breeding by the adults that are the most fit, the birth of the young when life is easiest, and maximum use of food when it is scarce.

ABOVE. *A herd of blue wildebeests*
(Connochaetes taurinus) *in flight across
the Serengeti Plain of Tanzania. Widely
dispersed during the rainy months, wildebeests
gather in tremendous assemblages of hundreds
of thousands in the dry season, moving forever
about, single-file, seeking water and pasture.
The wildebeest is a favorite prey of lions,
hyenas, and wild dogs, and predators may
claim eight out of every ten calves before
they reach maturity.*

An important element of this seasonal change is often the territorial behavior of the males. Among the herds, territoriality varies considerably among species, and even individuals, in the amount of territory claimed and how long it is held, and even whether or not they hold territory. Generally, however, territoriality is strongest when the land is lush, weakest during periods when animals are hard-pressed just to stay alive.

Once a male has established a territory, and as long as he holds it, he has the sole right to mate with the groups of females that wander into it in quest of food. The males that have the best pasturage in their territories retain the females the longest. An ample supply of food near at hand is also a tremendous advantage for the male as well, because between defending his land and winning the favor of females he has little time to feed.

The withering of the food supply as the dry season approaches sends the males farther and farther away from their little kingdoms in search of something to eat. The dominant males lose interest in maintaining their realms. Eventually, especially if the drought is severe, all defense is abandoned and the territorial system evaporates, as though carried away by the wind that whistles dryly through the acacia thorns.

For most of the herding, hoofed multitudes, the onset of hostile environmental conditions is followed by the disappearance of territorial behavior, a lowering of aggression, and the urge to gather with others of their kind. It happens to the huge gaurs of southern Asia during particularly severe droughts, and to the African buffaloes, which gather on the sides of hills and valleys when the dust devils swirl over the landscape. When the rains cease in East Africa, the Thomson's gazelles, which have been fiercely territorial, herd and migrate from the open plains to the bush in search of fresh pastures and water. On the steppes of Eurasia, the coming of winter ends the

OPPOSITE. *Armed with scimitar-shaped horns that may exceed five feet in length, the sable antelope (Hippotragus niger) fears not even a circling pride of lions. In the deciduous woodlands of South Africa, herds of up to 80 rust-colored females and their young range across the territories of several jet-black bulls.*

OVERLEAF. *A zebra cannot be mistaken for any other creature, but within the three species of zebras—indeed, within the most widely distributed species, the plains zebra (Equus burchellii)—there is great variation in the striping. Zebras find a certain amount of safety from their chief nemesis, the lion, by vigilance —they are very alert. While their primary defense in an attack is speed—up to 40 miles an hour—the stallion's hooves and teeth are weapons to make a lion wary.*

SECOND OVERLEAF. *Sharing the North American plains with the bison when the white man pushed into the western frontier were an estimated 40 million pronghorns (Antilocapra americana). They were not in competition for forage: bison graze the grasses, pronghorns browse shrubs and weeds. Nor did they deplete their pastures, for both species are nomads. There is no faster animal in the New World than the pronghorn: it can maintain a cruising speed of 30 miles an hour over several miles, with bursts up to 40 miles an hour. But it is unable to jump man's barbed-wire fences, and when the wild grass-lands were claimed for cattle, the pronghorn population plummeted, reaching a low of 30,000 in the 1920s. Conservation measures have restored pronghorn numbers somewhat, but even so they amount to only one percent of the size of the historic herds. The prong-horn's horn is unique in the mammal king-dom: the bony permanent core is covered with a hard sheath of fused hairs that is shed annually and consumed by rodents.*

LEFT. *Both male and female oryx (Oryx gazella) sport ringed, rapierlike horns, and those of the female are the longer, jutting up to four feet. If attacked by a lion, the oryx lowers its head and directs its men-acing weapons forward; and in territorial disputes, stabbing fights are common, although the thick hide over the upper body provides some protection from fatal injuries. So sharp are the horns of this large, beauti-fully marked antelope—scattered about Africa and Arabia in several subspecies— that natives use the tips as spear points.*

OPPOSITE. *The kob (Kobus kob) inhabits open grasslands of west and central Africa near swamps and rivers into which it can retreat to escape midday heat. Some kobs establish breeding arenas, within which each male has a circular territory 60 to 200 feet across. With whistling, stamping, and posturing, the male kob displays to and mates with any female that enters his particular field.*

OVERLEAF. *Whether a solitary bull sharply outlined by the morning sun on the South Dakota prairie, or a herd huddled against pelting snow and subzero cold, the American bison (Bison bison) is a living legend—and a reminder of how close we came to a great tragedy. Once there were 50 million bison on the Great Plains; by 1889, when the market hunters gave up their notorious slaughter, only 541 animals remained! An aroused public succeeded in protecting the survivors, and today there are 25,000 American bison roaming semi-free in the large national parks and wild-life refuges that preserve parts of their historic range. This is the largest land mammal in the New World; a bull, standing five feet at the shoulders, can weigh 1800 pounds. But the cow, although smaller, is more important to the youngster. A cow will nurse its single calf for an entire year, and the young bison will remain with its mother until it is sexually mature at the age of three years.*

SECOND OVERLEAF. *Weighing 1800 pounds and carrying five-foot horns, the African buffalo (Syncerus caffer) has a reputation—at least partly deserved—as the continent's most dangerous animal. Although it is normally peaceable, a wounded buffalo will lie in ambush for a hunter, and an old bull may stalk and charge a man without provocation. Oxpeckers are constantly in attendance on these wild cattle, ridding them of the torment of blood-sucking ticks.*

vicious territorial combats of the male saiga antelopes. The bulbous-nosed saigas merge into immense herds that run before the wind when blizzards sweep down from Siberia.

Nonherding browsers, such as the dik-dik, live in small home ranges that can be defended as year-round territories, but the great mixed herds are nomadic, and males cannot defend an immovable patch of ground for long. Only with the disappearance of territoriality can creatures such as the saigas form great, mixed herds. When the wildebeests migrate, for instance, males inspired by the territorial urge leave the main herds for a day or so, establish their transitory rule, mate with whatever females they can corral, and then return to the main body of antelopes. In contrast, the plains zebra, which often travels with the wildebeest and is dependent upon the same pastures, maintains a form of society that does not change with shifting environmental conditions. For the zebra, survival is best served by living year round in small family groups dominated by a king stallion, although stallions also live together in bachelor groups.

For the creatures such as the impala and hartebeest, the cyclic phenomenon of territoriality is just one of the factors that assures that the bulk of the young will be sired by the finest of the males and that the offspring will be born at a time when their chances of survival are highest. The young conceived at the height of the mating season will appear when there is plenty of pasturage, first for their mothers, who consequently can supply sufficient milk, and later for the newly weaned offspring. Moreover, having large numbers of young born at the same time guarantees that a sizable proportion will survive the ravages of predators, which, after all, kill just enough to satisfy their own needs. The young born late, however, have considerably less chance of surviving, not only because of a depleted food supply but also because the predators, no longer luxuriating in an overabundance of prey, pick them off one at a time.

Brutally efficient, the system nevertheless works out for the best interests of all species concerned.

The Domesticated Ones

On the Mediterranean coast of France, just west of Marseille, the two forks of the Rhone River flow to the sea in a welter of marshes, mudflats, and shallow lagoons. This vast delta region, known as the Camargue, is a land of beauty, strange and almost alien in aspect. Wild boars slosh through the shallows. Amphibians and reptiles swarm in freshwater marshes. Foxes skirt the salt lagoons where — astonishingly — vast flocks of greater flamingos congregate. And over this curious landscape roam herds of fierce black cattle and wild free horses, many almost white as snow.

The horses and cattle of the Camargue are domestic animals, but over long years they have been allowed to roam relatively free of interference. For all purposes, the cattle and horses of the Camargue are feral, reverted to an untamed state and living much as their wild ancestors did in prehistoric times. They are a reminder of the close links between many domestic creatures and their wild forebears and of how recently, in the long course of mammalian evolution, man has shaped domestic breeds. The domestic horse, for instance, was bred at least 4000 years ago from the wild horse which ranged the steppes of the Ukraine. The only wild horse that may be alive today is Przewalski's horse of Mongolia, but some scientists believe it, too, may be extinct. The other wild representatives of the family are zebras and asses. The horses of the Camargue, like the mustangs of the American West, are not wild in the strict sense, but actually are a domestic strain that has run free for 2000 years.

In the course of domestication, the traits that have made for manageability have been accentuated, and those that pose inconvenience or downright danger to humans have been eliminated by selective breeding. Thus it is that the male domestic yak is half the size of its rare wild relative, which weighs more than a thousand pounds. Similarly, most donkeys are smaller than the pony-sized North African wild ass, their graceful, fleet ancestor, and many strains of domestic

OPPOSITE. *The only surviving race of truly wild horses is the endangered Przewalski's horse, which was once widely distributed across Asia. About two hundred of its kind are found in zoos around the world, and it is barely possible that a few still exist in the Gobi Desert of China and Mongolia. The so-called wild horses that range the western plains of North America are feral descendants of cowboys' steeds. And the Camargue horses that splash across the shallow lagoons of that marshy island on the Rhone delta of France likewise are domestic animals gone wild, although they are a fairly recent descendant of a wild horse that was crossed with Oriental blood.*

OVERLEAF AND SECOND OVERLEAF. *The alpaca and llama are domesticated forms of New World camels; two other kinds, the guanaco and vicuña, survive in a wild state in the South American Andes. The exact lineage of the alpaca and llama — indeed, even whether they should be considered true species — is a mystery that probably will plague science forever. Neither the alpaca nor the llama existed in the wild when the Spanish conquistadores arrived, and archaeological discoveries suggest they had been tamed and bred many centuries before the Inca Empire, probably from the wild guanaco. Moreover, all four New World camels interbreed and produce fertile offspring.*

water buffalo are considerably less bulky than the wild variety, and have less imposing horns, sometimes none at all.

The water buffalo has been harnessed for use because of its adaptability to a very special set of environmental circumstances. It can be used for milk production, and more importantly as a beast of burden, in the hot, swampy places that are all but unlivable for domestic cattle and oxen. Because the water buffalo can work in the mud and water of rice paddies, marshes, and jungles, it has gained in numbers to perhaps 150 million animals worldwide. Water buffaloes have been spread to such diverse lands as Italy, Brazil, and Australia, running feral in parts of the latter two countries.

The same adaptability to quite special surroundings characterizes several other domestic ungulates. The yak, the llama, and the alpaca are all suited for the windswept reaches of the high mountains. All have been developed from beasts that evolved on arid tableland up to altitudes of 17,000 feet, and even higher in the case of the yak. The llama, a beast of burden, and the alpaca, kept for its long, fine wool, descend from the far-ranging guanaco, which while it roams to the edge of the sea—and even to some islands—is very much a creature of the high, arid plains of the Andes. The yak's wild relative inhabits the wind-whipped deserts of northern Tibet, a bleak, barren wilderness. The country inhabited by these animals, and in which their domestic relatives are employed, represents some of the most difficult, dangerous terrain on earth, where surefootedness is at a premium and a capacity for subsisting on tough, sparse vegetation is essential. The shaggy winter coats that serve the guanaco and wild yak so well under near-glacial conditions have become in their domesticated relatives a source of extremely useful wool. Selective breeding, for example, has produced alpacas with fringes of wool so long they nearly brush the ground; the long, thin wool is considered to be among the world's finest and is extremely valuable.

BELOW. *A herd of Indian wild asses (*Equus hemionus khur*) on the Little Rann of Kutch, a vast salt-impregnated wasteland near the Pakistan frontier. This is one of five subspecies of the Asiatic wild ass; one race, in Syria, is feared extinct, and all the others are considered rare. Competition from domestic livestock for badly overgrazed forage, uncontrolled slaughter for its meat and because its testes were thought to be a powerful aphrodisiac, and its capture for uses as a draught animal exterminated the Indian wild ass from most of its historic range. But a thousand wild asses still survive on the Little Rann of Kutch, which lies only a foot or two above the Arabian Sea; there they have been rigorously protected for decades. Moreover, local people are strict vegetarians.*

The mountaineering abilities of the guanaco, its domestic descendants, and, for that matter, its close wild relative the vicuña, extend even to their metabolic processes. Their blood cells, small compared to those of humans, are numerous, providing a greater capacity to carry oxygen. Moreover, the hemoglobin in their blood has a relatively high affinity for oxygen, further boosting the talent these creatures have for operating under full speed at altitudes where exertion would leave many other animals gasping.

The guanaco, llama, alpaca, and vicuña belong to a family noted for its toughness and ability to get along under the most difficult conditions. The Old World members of the group, the camels, carry out the tradition in the deserts. Both of the two types of domestic camel can negotiate the most parched wastelands, the two-humped or Bactrian camel where it is cold, the one-humped or dromedary in regions where it is searingly hot. The endurance of the camel without water in the desert is legendary; the reasons for it are not fully understood. It seems, however, that the camel lasts so long without drinking because it uses water with nearly ultimate efficiency. Its urine is highly concentrated, but that is not particularly unique for desert animals. The camel, though, has other, rather unusual adaptations for living in the hot waterless places. Its woolly coat insulates it from the sun's heat. It can lower its body temperature during the cool desert night to as low as 90° F. It warms up slowly, and it is not until its body temperature exceeds 104° F. that it must begin to cool down. It can obtain water from its food, especially in the cooler winter when one can go months without drinking. Legends of water stored in the hump or stomach are untrue. For thousands of years—perhaps six thousand in the case of the dromedary—the camel's toughness and ability to withstand heat and lack of water have enabled the people who live with it to survive in regions that otherwise would not be populated by humans.

ABOVE. *The Altai Mountains rise in the distance as a herd of wild two-humped camels* (Camelus bactrianus) *crosses the Gobi Desert of Mongolia. There are two species of Old World camels, the one-humped dromedary, which originally came from Arabia, and the two-humped Bactrian camel from Chinese Turkestan and Mongolia. Both have been widely domesticated as beasts of burden, and only the Bactrian camel still survives in a wild population — numbering about 900 animals on both sides of the China-Mongolia border. In summer, the wild camels climb into the mountains as high as 11,000 feet to escape the heat, returning to the grassy steppes and desert in winter. Traveling in groups of perhaps twenty females and young, led by a male, they forage in the morning and evening for grass, herbs, branches, and, in autumn, the fallen leaves of poplar trees. Heavy hunting for its meat and hides, and competition from domestic animals for scarce water and pasture, are blamed for the wild camel's decline. But this rare species is now strictly protected by both nations.*

Unique Giants

OPPOSITE. *When a bull hippopotamus (Hippopotamus amphibius) opens its cavernous mouth in a "yawn," exposing sharp incisors and huge lower canine tusks that may be twenty-five inches long, it is not a sign of laziness. By showing off the formidable weapons that jut from its powerful jaws, the hippo is trying to intimidate a rival. But such threat displays as often as not incite rather than prevent fights, and a battle between two hippos can be awesome and bloody. For an hour or two the hippos rush at each other with gaping mouths, sending waves rushing across the lake or river as they attempt to drive those great canine teeth — once used to make human dentures — through the thick hide and into the heart of their opponent.*

High upon Kenya's Aberdare Mountains, towering almost 13,000 feet into the equatorial sky, lie rolling moorlands, swept by winds that play with the mist clouds and fray their edges to shreds. Scattered about the moors are outcrops of rock and, breaking up the expanses of low vegetation, thickets of giant heath, taller than a man and bearded with lichens.

The gray-green vegetation of the thickets has a ravaged look, as if torn and splintered by some immensely powerful force. That, in fact, is exactly what has happened, for elephants climb the steep, slick trails into the highlands and feed in the foggy heath groves. Unable to jump, the elephants nevertheless are agile enough to climb the steep slopes that separate the moorlands from the forest below. Once they gain the top, they bulldoze into the thickets, white tusks gleaming amidst the dark foliage. The sight evokes images of Pleistocene times, some 50,000 years ago, when pachyderms roamed subglacial landscapes quite similar to the rolling uplands of the Aberdares. In the world of nature, size is a signal advantage for a herbivorous creature; colossal bulk and the strength that goes with it can render a creature such as the elephant invulnerable to any land predator. But today the very size of the elephants and a few other giants has become a liability, because space is at a premium, especially where these giants live. With the possible exception of the giraffe, the last giants have been pushed by expanding human populations into a few fragile havens in the jungles of Southeast Asia and the forests and grasslands of Africa.

In the swampy grasslands and jungles of the Kaziranga National Park of Assam, India, and in the Royal Chitawan National Park of Nepal, live most of the world's 1,950 great Indian rhinos. Like the Javan species, its close cousin, the Indian rhino is armored with heavy plates of thick skin, joined by thin folds that permit graceful, free movement. Given to frequent squabbles, Indian rhinos fight each other with slashing, and often fatal, swipes of incisors lengthened into razor-sharp tusks. The Indian rhino seldom employs its horn, which, as in other rhinos, is not a

149

true horn with a bony core but is made of matted keratin fibers, like the material that forms a hoof. Perhaps because the Indian rhino prolongs its spectacularly violent mating act for the better part of an hour, rhino horn, from all species, is prized in Asian folk medicine as an aphrodisiac. This belief is unfortunate, for it makes rhinos a prime target for poachers; and today, all five rhino species are endangered. In most Asian cities with large Chinese populations, one can find, in medicine shops, rhino horns from India and Africa. Indian rhino horn, the most expensive of the two, now sells in Hong Kong for as much as $9000 per pound wholesale, and $30,000 retail.

Both African rhinos, the black and the white or square-lipped, carry two horns, which may reach a yard or more in length. Weighing up to 5000 pounds, the white rhino is the largest living rhinoceros, but a hornless rhino of about 30 million years ago towered twice as high and may have been the largest mammal ever to walk the earth.

The windswept thorn scrub of Kenya and Tanzania is the heart of black rhino country, but even there, this myopic beast is severely endangered. Perhaps fewer than 4500 remain in Africa and they depend almost entirely on sanctuaries.

Rhinos often share their sanctuaries with the colossus among the giants, the African elephant of the bush country. A big bush elephant can reach six tons in weight and thirteen feet at the shoulder. A slow-motion study in violence, the advance of an elephant herd eating its way through a grove of acacias in the African bush is unhurried but inexorable, and guaranteed to make a watcher feel puny, so casually do the great beasts commit acts of Herculean destruction. The elephants' great trunks, whose two-fingered tips are sensitive enough to pick up a peanut, gently wrap around sturdy tree limbs, then tear them away more easily than a man could pluck a rose. If leaves are too high, the trees that bear them are nudged by broad gray foreheads until wood splinters and

OPPOSITE AND PAGE 153. *Worrying the desiccated remains of one of its own, ripping apart an acacia tree to obtain part of the 300 pounds of food it requires every day, bathing with dust—all are routines in the daily life of the African elephant (Loxodonta africana), the largest land mammal on earth. In particular, elephants spend a great deal of time washing, powdering, and massaging their skin, which is unusually sensitive for a beast that weighs six tons.*

they crash to the ground. An African elephant can consume up to 600 pounds of vegetation daily, so not surprisingly, when confined to parks, elephants literally eat themselves out of a home. Their destructive feeding has become an increasingly critical problem in Africa.

The African elephant's tusks, elongated upper incisors that grow throughout life, can reach a length of a dozen feet. Although nominally outlawed, killing of elephants for their tusks goes on in most of their African range, with the ivory going to markets in Hong Kong and mainland China. Of itself, the poaching might not imperil the existence of the species, but in the face of declining habitat, the African elephant cannot long endure the poisoned arrows and traps of poachers.

The hippopotamus of Africa also carries formidable tusks, which are not incisors but canines in the lower jaw. When angered, the hippo opens its jaws in a cavernous yawn, baring its huge weapons, which it can wield with lethal effectiveness. Most of the time, however, hippos are the picture of luxuriant loafing, particularly during the day. Bunched together in the mud like hogs, they bask on sandbanks, their dark hides tinged red by protective mucus, secreted by glands in the skin.

After dark, however, the hippo is transformed. It heaves its body from the water and, leaving its platter-sized, four-toed prints in the mud, briskly heads overland. Along age-old trails, hippos may travel miles to their feeding plots. In the course of a night, 100 pounds of grass and other fodder can disappear down the maw of a single large hippo. If farmers have planted crops on hippo feeding grounds, the devastation is swift, and so is the reprisal. The last terrestrial giants have no way of knowing that they evolved in a world when humans were scattered and few, and no plow had broken the earth. They cannot know that the days when they were lords of the land are over, and that their fate is now entirely in the hands of a pygmy called man.

OVERLEAF. *With its hind feet reaching ahead of the front feet and its long neck swinging like a pendulum, the giraffe* (Giraffa camelo-pardalis) *can lope tirelessly across the East African plains at speeds of up to 30 miles an hour. Running is the giraffe's primary defense against its only natural enemy, the lion, but if cornered it can crush the big cat's skull with blows from its front legs.*

SECOND OVERLEAF. *A single horn and thickly folded, tubercle-covered skin that gives it an armored appearance identify the great Indian rhinoceros* (Rhinoceros unicornis). *Fewer than two thousand of these endangered giants still survive in sanctuaries in India and Nepal. Weighing two and a half tons, the great Indian rhinoceros is the second largest of the five species of rhino found in Africa and Asia. The female bears a single calf after a gestation period of sixteen months, and the newborn rhino weighs 200 pounds and has all the skin folds and rivetlike protuberances of an adult, lacking only the nose horn. Over its first year of life, drinking twenty-five quarts of milk a day from its mother, the calf will multiply its weight tenfold at the rate of six pounds a day. It will not be weaned until it is two and a half years old.*

Life on the Peaks

Although many mammals roam the world's high places, one group of horned, hoofed creatures in particular has made the windswept, stony heights its special playground. Native in one form or another to Eurasia, northern Africa, and North America, the goats, sheep, and a few related beasts clatter over all but the very highest reaches of the mountains with a wild freedom that makes them seem kin to the wind. Superbly equipped for life atop the crags, these mountaineering mammals feed, breed, and even rear their young on landscapes of incredible harshness. The four-chambered stomachs of these ruminants can glean enough nourishment from rubbery scrub, wisps of grass, and scraps of lichen to thrive in the marginal environment of the peaks, where other large mammals would starve.

Amazingly sure of foot, these creatures of the alpine solitudes have a dizzying aptitude for cavorting on eminences above the clouds. Persian wild goats leap about the boulders almost 14,000 feet up in the barren mountains west of the Caspian Sea, where Iran, the Soviet Union, and Turkey meet. The big Siberian ibex goes even higher and, like others of its species, easily perches on any pinnacle with enough room for its four feet. Bighorn sheep survey the Rocky Mountains from lookouts 10,000 feet high. In the Himalayas, blue sheep—not exactly true sheep and not blue, either, but gray—loll on grassy slopes at 18,000 feet.

Of them all, however, the true king of the mountain is the North American mountain goat, a bearded will-o'-the-wisp as white as the snow that swirls about its native western mountains in the winter. Once sighted in the heights, the goats are given to vanishing with ghostly abruptness, then suddenly reappearing at the edge of even higher peaks. The mountain goat is not a true goat, but along with its cousins the Eurasian chamois, and the serows and gorals of Asia, is considered relatively primitive. True goats (and sheep) are recently evolved and have long curving horns. Scientists have trouble classifying some of the mountaineering mammals. The blue sheep, for instance, is actually a sheep-like goat who was put alone in its genus. In the end, its name is based upon its general appearance.

The backgrounds against which the mountain goat is pictured tell much about the brutal conditions with which it must cope. Unlike the bighorns, which descend to the shelter of lower slopes in the autumn, and the corkscrew-horned markhor goats of Asia, which emerge from the heights to feed on live oak when the snow flies, the mountain goats seldom stray below the timberline. There are exceptions, of course, but mountain goats generally head for the trees only in the spring, when the sweet, green shoots lure them from their high havens. The goats negotiate the steep slopes and sheer, gray headwalls of their world with stiff-legged deliberation, pausing frequently to consider the next move. Traveling this way a goat can ascend nearly vertical palisades, when necessary pulling its 300-pound body from ledge to ledge with its black hooves. If a goat reaches a dead-end ledge, it rears upon its hind legs, whirls about, and returns the way it came, often by stupendous leaps

BELOW. *The master of a harem of bighorn ewes routs a young rival. Negotiating such precipitous cliffs is not a great challenge for a mountain sheep. Its hoof has a hard outer edge and toe that grips in loose dirt or rock cracks, plus a resilient pad at the back that provides traction on smooth surfaces. Moreover, to the ram's eye there usually are well-defined, if zigzag, paths across such jagged rock faces. And if not, the bighorn can plunge down a rock chute, hurtling from niche to niche in a controlled fall with the ease that comes from superb traction and balance.*

from rock to rock. The fancy footwork of the goat is due in large measure to the structure of its hooves; it and the other members of the group have two on each foot. In the center of each hoof is a spongy, elastic pad, like a tire tread, which provides traction, while the hard-edged rim of the hoof catches in minute clefts and crevices—an arrangement shared by other mountain mammals.

The chamois, which roves mountain ranges from the Pyrenees to the Caucasus, and has been transplanted to New Zealand, is more graceful than its American relative. But it has the same uncanny ability to materialize seemingly out of nowhere. One moment a talus slope appears empty, the next a chamois is there, scanning the slopes below. If it senses danger, however, the chamois moves with dazzling speed, leaping and bounding over chasms so lightly it seems to fly. If cornered, a chamois fights with vicious thrusts of its foot-long horns, but rarely are these weapons used so murderously as in rutting battles between the males.

Chamois, and mountain goats, sometimes fight to the death in such combats, and once the weaker duelist gives ground, he may be pursued ferociously, even knocked spinning from a cliff. Male mountain goats, moreover, do not reserve their aggressiveness for other adult males, but are notorious kid killers, perhaps the worst enemies of their own young.

The rutting combats of most other animals in this group, on the other hand, are ritualized to prevent serious injury and death. The crash of bighorns hammering against each other's huge, curled horns sometimes can be heard a mile away—but the blows are always horn on horn. The horns also armor their owners against even pile-driving blows, which also are cushioned by the skull. Bighorns have a tendency, like an experienced boxer, to "roll with the punch." Males with horns markedly different in size seldom fight.

The males of most of the true sheep and goats carry horns that are massive in relation to their body size. The Nubian ibex, found in Israel and the Sinai, as well as Africa, has horns almost four feet long. Yet this smallest of ibexes is not much more than knee-high to a man at its shoulder. The Persian wild goat, which weighs up to 198 pounds, has saber-shaped horns that sometimes reach a length of more than five feet. And even a mouflon, little more than two feet high at the shoulder, can have horns a yard long.

The most impressive horns of all, however, belong to the argali sheep, an awesome creature four feet high at the shoulder, larger than a bighorn. Some argalis carry horns six feet long that, flaring outward in a wide spiral, approach six feet from tip to tip. The argalis inhabit some of the bleakest mountains in the world, in the cold interior of central Asia, and in their isolation are symbolic of all the mountain animals, for they are creatures of a world that, until recently, existed on a plane above humanity. As long as the mountaineering mammals remain in the wild, they are assurance that somewhere on this earth, a living creature remains in splendid isolation.

Mammals in the Sea

Watching a great whale rise from the depths of a calm sea is like witnessing the birth of an island. One moment the sea is smooth, stirred only by light swells that slide gently across its surface, or perhaps by the occasional splash of a seabird knifing into the water after a fish. Then the ocean parts. A dark and mountainous form, encrusted with a white mottling of barnacles, heaves above the surface. Water drains in torrents from the crest of its back and sluices into the foam boiling around it. Overhead, like clouds of steam above a volcano, hangs the condensation from the sea beast's exhalations, which fill the air with a mighty rushing sound. It is an experience to make one feel fragile and insignificant, and to prompt pondering about man's place on earth.

The great whales are the most spectacular of a group of mammals that have adapted to the world of water. This assemblage also includes the smaller whales, dolphins, and porpoises, the seals and their kin, and the dugongs and manatees. In a sense, they have come full circle, for they have returned to the environment from which their remote cold-blooded ancestors crept and, indeed, from which all life arose. Most of them are marine, but a few, such as the weak-eyed river dolphins of Asia and South America, and Siberia's Lake Baikal seal, spend their lives in fresh water. Although the mammals here belong to three unrelated orders, they share a parallel history. For reasons only to be surmised, the ancestors forsook the land and committed themselves to life in the water—probably because the pressures of competition or the need for a new source of food forced them to. The whales, dolphins, and porpoises—together called cetaceans —made the transition in the Eocene Period, at the dawn of the Age of Mammals more than 45 million years ago. The dugongs and manatees, comprising the order of sirenians, accomplished it at about the same time. Not for another 20 million years, in the Miocene Period, did the seals, sea lions, and walruses appear in the sea. They were grouped together in a single order, the pinnipeds—meaning "wing-footed"—but all three families did not evolve from the same ancestor. The true seals, streamlined

OPPOSITE. *Each wartlike knob on the head of this humpback calf contains a single sensitive vibrissa that is similar to a cat's whisker. The baby whale, sixteen feet long at birth, is not yet parasitized by the barnacles that bedeck adult humpbacks—as much as a half ton of them affixed to a single whale.*

169

LEFT. *Sea lions* (Zalophus californianus wollebaeki) *soak up the equatorial sun burning down on the Galápagos lava. Unlike fur seals, sea lions were not hunted primarily for their pelts, since their coat has no underfur. Instead, they were slaughtered for food and rendered for oil and their skins were processed into low-grade leather.*

BELOW. *Skilled swimmers, sea lions can dive to depths of nearly 300 feet and remain submerged for five minutes or longer. But deadly enemies are waiting offshore: sharks and killer whales.*

TOP LEFT. *Harp seals (Phoca groenlandica) are true seals that move on land only with considerable difficulty. Their annual oceanic migrations cover 6000 miles, and scientists calculate that a harp seal must consume a ton and a half of fish and crustaceans to fuel its journey. Harp seals bear their young on pack ice off the coasts of Labrador, Newfoundland, and Greenland, and the slaughter of newborn pups for their pure-white coats is a continuing source of international controversy.*

TOP RIGHT. *Soon after the birth of her single pup, which weighs less than five pounds, a sea lion cow will mate again. The pups, which bleat like lambs, spend their first four months nursing and frolicking in tidal pools. The mortality rate is high: pups often fall into the sea, are unable to scramble back onto the rocks, and drown; others are crushed by bulls fighting over females.*

BOTTOM. *The aptly named leopard seal (Hydrurga leptonyx) patrols Antarctic ice floes, waiting for Adelie penguins to enter the water. Its prey is quickly dispatched, shaken out of its skin, and swallowed piecemeal, mostly just the flesh. So fierce that they are avoided even by packs of killer whales, leopard seals are longer than all other seals except the elephant seal. Powerful swimmers, they are able to shoot out of the water and land on ice eight feet above.*

OVERLEAF. *Two walrus calves nuzzle each other, showing the stiff bristles that, when they begin to fend for themselves after nursing for two years, will be an important tool in feeding. They use these sensitive bristles to locate food on muddy bottoms by touch. Young walruses also begin foraging for clams and other small shellfish at six months. While they are weaned completely at two years old, young male walruses will continue to follow their mother for two to four more years; young females will follow their mother even longer—sometimes for life.*

for swimming to the degree that they have lost external ears, have an otter-like ancestor. The fur seals, sea lions, and walruses, on the other hand, descended from creatures close to bears. Thus they are now grouped with other carnivores.

The ways in which these creatures have adapted to life beyond the world's shorelines merit profound consideration, if not awe, because they all have managed to cope with an environment almost as hostile to a mammal as the cold blackness of space.

As a matter of course, these animals go for long periods without breathing the air upon which they, like all other mammals, depend. The sirenians sometimes stay below for a quarter of an hour as they pull eelgrass, water hyacinths, and other aquatic plants into their small mouths with the aid of a fleshy and flexible upper lip. The sea otter scours the bottom down to one hundred feet, probing with stubby fingers for the shellfish and sea urchins it relishes. A month-old harbor seal can dive for up to four minutes on a single breath. A yearling of the same species can hold its breath for twenty minutes. When necessary, as in a titanic battle with a huge squid, the legendary sperm whale can remain under water for an hour and a half.

To remain under very long without breathing, a sea mammal must use oxygen with exceptional economy, and in fact this ability is one of the traits unifying the orders which have left the land behind. The sirenians and whales promote oxygen conservation with their relatively low metabolism. In terms of calories per kilogram of body weight, the basic metabolic rate of a whale is one-fifteenth that of a human, and the blood of a typical whale holds sufficient oxygen to keep its bodily processes going for more than an hour. Sea mammals also have an abundance of myoglobin, the oxygen-carrying protein that serves the same function in the muscles as hemoglobin in the blood. It all means that their bodies store vast amounts of oxygen.

Even more telling is the astonishing efficiency with which sea mammals operate during a dive. They reduce, even shut off, all bodily activities not essential beneath the surface of the water. By selected constriction of the blood vessels, the flow to the kidneys and digestive system, for example, is slowed drastically, while blood continues to rush unimpeded to the brain, spinal cord, and heart muscles. Beyond this, the sea mammals seem rather insensitive to the buildup of carbon dioxide, which in land mammals quickly triggers impulses in the respiratory center of the brain that result in the act of taking breath.

The ability to clamp the nostrils tightly shut underwater, closing off the respiratory system, is an enormous advantage for a mammal in the water. For this purpose, the nostrils of pinnipeds are narrow slits. Those of the sirenians and cetaceans are round orifices ringed by a muscular rim. Moreover, the nostrils of cetaceans have been moved from the snout to the apex of the head, forming a single blowhole in the toothed

whales, paired in the baleen whales. As a result, a whale can breathe with only the tip of its head above the surface.

Many other changes, some quite obvious, have occurred in those mammals that truly have made the water their home. Most recognizable is that they have taken on the so-called fusiform body shape typical of fish, at its sleekest, perhaps, in creatures such as the killer whale. Even such bulky and ponderous animals as the walrus and dugong streamline into a torpedo shape as they move through the water. The density of water has had other influences on the sea mammals. Only the aquatic environment could produce an animal with a body more than 100 feet long, weighing 170 tons. That creature is the blue whale, the largest animal that has ever lived. Ironically, the blue whale may vanish because of its size, which marked this mighty sea mammal as a prime target of whalers—men as rapacious as many of the beasts under the sea.

TOP LEFT. *The northern elephant seal* (Mirounga angustirostris) *of California waters nearly passed into extinction in the 1890s. By the time it was given complete protection from hunting in 1912, fewer than 100 animals survived. Today there are 50,000, most on the Channel Islands off Los Angeles. The northern species has a longer "trunk" than its Antarctic cousin—that snout that dangles limp most of the year but is inflated during the excitement of the mating season. Elephant seals haul out on land twice a year—once to breed, and again a few weeks later to molt. While ashore they fast, living off their great fat reserves built up by feasting on cuttlefish and squid caught in the ocean depths.*

TOP RIGHT. *The ivory tusks of a walrus* (Odobenus rosmarus) *grow throughout the animal's life, and those of a mature male can reach a length of forty inches and weigh twelve pounds. The walrus uses its tusks to haul its two-ton hulk out of the sea, to chop breathing holes in ice, and to fight with rivals or display dominance status.*

TOP. *A 1500-pound West Indian manatee* (Trichechus manatus) *can remain submerged for sixteen minutes as it feasts on aquatic vegetation. It pushes plants toward its mouth with its flippers and picks them up with a split lip that is used like a forceps. In cold weather, Florida's manatees congregate around the mouths of warmer rivers and even hydroelectric outflows in Miami.*

BOTTOM. *In the clear waters off the Hawaiian islands of Maui, a calf humpback whale* (Megaptera novaeangliae) *stays close by the side of its mother. Some two hundred of these rare whales, famous for their "singing," use the warm near-shore waters of Hawaii as a mating ground and as a nursery, remaining there from February to June, when they depart for nutrient-rich feeding grounds in cold northern seas.*

OVERLEAF. *At sunset on Hood Island, a Galápagos sea lion cow and her calf luxuriate in the falling spray from a blowhole. Like fur seals, sea lions belong to the family of eared seals. They can stand on four "legs" and almost gallop on land.*

SECOND OVERLEAF. *A common dolphin* (Delphinus delphis) *races alongside a yacht in the Galápagos Islands. Eight feet long, capable of attaining a speed of 30 miles an hour, this is truly the common dolphin of temperate seas around the world; herds of Delphinus numbering in the thousands can literally churn the ocean to froth as they pursue squid, baitfish, and flying fish.*

THIRD OVERLEAF. *In a burst of spray, a southern right whale* (Balaena australis) *explodes from a bay off Punta Váldez on the coast of Argentina, hurling itself into the air with such momentum that it somersaults. A whale will breach repeatedly, a score or more times, always landing on its back or side with a thunderous whack. Just why whales breach is not understood; it may be done to dislodge parasites —or just for sport.*

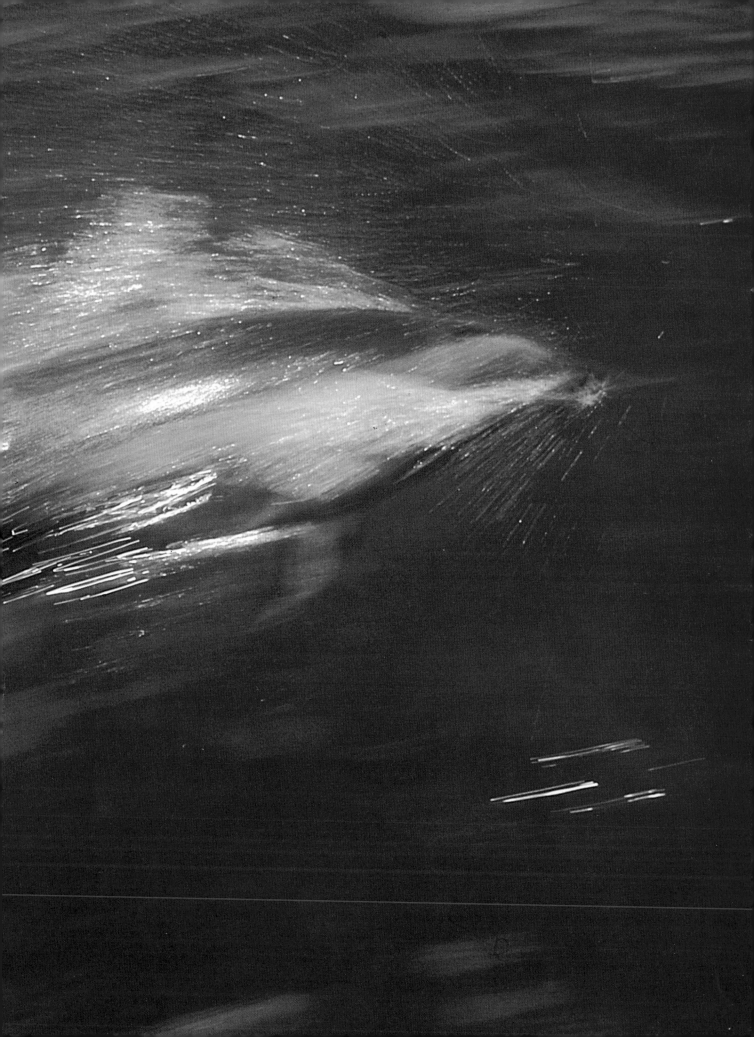

Photo Credits

Les Line began his career as a newspaper reporter, photographer, and columnist in Michigan. He served as editor of *Audubon* magazine from 1966–91, transforming it into what Roger Tory Peterson called "not only the most beautiful natural history magazine in the world, but the most beautiful magazine of any sort in the English language." Line, the author of several books, is a regular contributor to many magazines and newspapers such as *National Wildlife* and *The New York Times*.

Edward R. Ricciuti, formerly curator of publications for the New York Zoological Society, is the author of more than fifty books, including *The Audubon Society Book of Wild Cats* and *Wildlife of the Mountains,* as well as many articles in major magazines and newspapers. He is a consultant to zoos, aquariums, and conservation organizations, and has done field research in Africa, Southeast Asia, South America, Iran, the Middle East, and Yugoslavia.